How I Write
The Secret Lives of Authors

First
published
in the
United States
of America
in 2007 by
Rizzoli
International
Publications, Inc.
300 Park
Avenue South
New York,
NY 10010
www.rizzoliusa.com
How I Write:
The Secret
Lives
of Authors,
edited by
Dan Crowe
with Philip
Oltermann
© 2007
the authors
Library
of Congress
Control Number:
2006906709
2007 2008 2009 /
10 9 8 7 6 5 4 3 2 1
Printed in China
ISBN:
0-8478-
2942-1
ISBN-13:
978-0-8478-
2942-2

How I Write
The Secret Lives of Authors

Edited by Dan Crowe
With Philip Oltermann

"I had a close look at my desk just now and realized that it just wasn't designed for quality writing."

Franz Kafka's diary, 24 December 1910

Contents

Their maggots
and their butterflies
An introduction

In *Money* (1984), walking hangover and celluloid pimp John Self offers the reader an exclusive peek into the private world of his creator: "I tell you, this Martin Amis, he lives like a student. I had inspected his flat with an adman's eye, mindful of outlay and lifestyle, of vocational expenditure. And there was nothing, no tape recorders or filing cabinets or electric typewriters or word processors. Just his pastel portable, like an ancient till. Just biros, pads, pencils. Just two dust-furred rooms off a sooty square, with no hall or passage. And he earns enough. Why isn't he living right up to the hilt of his dough? He must have a bad book-habit, this character. How much are books? It seems he has the reading-thing real bad."

How I Write was born out of curiosity. Like John Self, we wanted to tear down the invisible wall between us readers and them writers and see what's really going on behind the page. What keeps writers going? If not money, what is their fix? What gets them high? What gets them low? Where do they get their ideas from? And what *do* they do all day?

And yet, with the curiosity also came guilt. The phrasing of our letter to the authors was awkward, clunky. Dear writer, it said. Can you think for a minute about which object, picture, or document in your study reveals most about the relationship between living and writing, and then send it to us?

Literature, we knew, wasn't meant to be about this. Literature was meant to be about big themes, great ideas, strong emotions. Good literature takes you on a journey into the wide world—we were asking writers to step back into the narrow confinement of their own four walls. How rude we were. And how "fetishistic," as one writer replied— as if we had just asked him to show us a picture of his grandmother wrapped in furs (remarkably, that picture arrived later, from a different writer). We felt like we had the adman's eye real bad. Maybe we shouldn't have been so worried. Writers through the ages have found that there can be a useful link between the fuzzy blur of ideas and the hard-edged particularity of objects. The wisest men in history, Laurence Sterne remarks in *The Life and Times of Tristram Shandy, Gentleman*, have always had "hobby-horses": "their coins and their cockle-shells, their

drums and their trumpets, their fiddles, their pallets, their maggots and their butterflies." A few examples. Agatha Christie used to get her best ideas whenever she was doing the dishes. Gore Vidal swears by coffee ("First coffee, then a bowel movement and then the muse joins me"). Lewis Carroll was devoted to tea, and would go to lengths to achieve the perfect brew—one visitor remembered him walking up and down his sitting room swaying the teapot to and fro for precisely ten minutes. For *A Clockwork Orange* author Anthony Burgess, it had to be alcohol, and in particular his own "Hangman's Blood" recipe (gin, whisky, rum, port, brandy, and stout, topped up with champagne). William Faulkner's routine included watching the 1960s television comedy *Car 54, Where are You?* every Sunday night. Whenever G.K. Chesterton had writer's block, he would take up his bow and fire arrows through his window at a tree in the garden until everything made sense again.

Dan Brown allegedly pauses at regular intervals for a few sit-ups, press-ups, and quick stretches to stimulate the blood-flow to the brain. Honoré de Balzac was addicted to a 15-hour working regime. Popular legend has it that Anthony Trollope was so particular about his routine of turning out exactly seven pages per day that even if he finished a novel by lunchtime, he'd put the title of a new novel on the next page and continue writing until he had reached his daily quota.

Sometimes the hobby-horse can be one particular physical object, rather than a general routine of doing things. James Joyce would always carry a ring made of various kinds of metal on his hand, which he superstitiously believed to be a preventative against blindness. Gustave Flaubert allegedly found it impossible to write a word unless his lover's mittens and slippers were resting in the drawer by his writing desk. Henrik Ibsen was more of a masochist: he kept a pet scorpion in his study. For some, the key to success was all in the furniture: Herman Melville used to write in a rocking chair in his Arrowhead home, facing Mount Greylock—Massachusetts's highest point—through the window. Jane Austen relied on a creaky door to warn her if someone was entering her room while she was writing, so that she could quickly hide small scraps of paper under a blotter. Philip Roth allegedly works at a lectern at right angles to a view of the Empire State Building—much like Thomas Wolfe, who wrote standing up, using the top of his fridge as a desk. Whenever Bruno Schulz was anxious—and he often was—he would draw the outline of a rudimentary house in the air.

Often these are no more than behavioral quirks. In most cases, they are irrelevant to the writers' art. But sometimes the object and the art it inspires are inseparable. Oscar Wilde, ever the aesthete, would keep Pre-Raphaelite lilies in his undergraduate room at Oxford, inside large vases of blue china. The vases are intrinsically linked to the first Wildean aphorism that achieved national currency: "I find it harder and harder every day to live up to my blue china."

When that other great wit of English letters, P.G. Wodehouse, was writing a book, he used to pin the pages of his manuscript in waves around the wall of his workroom. The good pages would go at the top—the unfinished ones would be stuck close to the floor, slowly working their way to eye level in reward for an additional joke here, an extra flourish there. "His aim," writes Douglas Adams in his essay on Wodehouse, "was to get the entire manuscript up to the picture rail before he handed it in." Vladimir Nabokov was perhaps the ultimate hobby-horse man: a fanatical (if scientifically naïve) collector of butterflies, he believed that pastimes can sharpen the eye for detail that makes a good writer.

But the relationship between the extraordinary universe of ideas and the pedestrian world of "things" is not always one of affiliation. Anyone who has ever fallen for the idea that clearing your writing space while writing might help—by association— to organize your thoughts, knows what it's like to suddenly find yourself in a perfectly tidy room without a single word having materialized on the page. The talisman that was meant to trigger your memory often triggers all but an avalanche of excuses for time-wasting.

There is a sinister message behind knick-knacks: why are you wasting your time with material pleasures? Tempus fugit! Time flies! Get on with the real thing! In the sixteenth century, people were crazy about collecting objects that symbolized transience: skulls, stuffed animals, pictures of wilting flowers. Material objects are always mementi mori: poignant reminders that our objects will outlive our thoughts. Whatever it was, something in our original letter must have struck a chord with the writers, because responses to our invites came thick and fast. The first was from writer and film director Bruce Robinson. He wasn't quite sure what we were after, he said. There was nothing of real interest in his study— to prove his point, he added a short description of his desk and the quotes he had stuck up on the wall, including one from James Joyce: "Write it damn you, what else are you good for." He apologized for not being able to get involved and wished us good luck. The letter, of course, was perfect: personal, real, humorous, something that offered a brief glimpse of the real person behind the words.

Some writers got the idea instantly. They would reveal to us that a single talisman had been key to their creative spark, all the way from their first short story to their biggest bestseller, and needed to be near them at all times. Others had whole desks, entire rooms full of little objects they had collected over the years—which one did we want? Others, again, didn't have a clue what we were talking about—they didn't "do" lucky charms. In those cases, we would keep on probing: there had to be something they did when they wanted to take a break from writing. Or something that helped them keep writers' block at bay. Someplace they turned to when they couldn't decide where their story should go next.

Emails would fly back and forth for months and months, until the subject headings looked like pathetic attempts to render into words the sound of an engine starting: Re: Re: Re: Re: Re: Re. In most cases, the ignition would catch eventually. We wanted a photo of their creaky chair? Of the shower? A pack of cigarettes? That Sinatra record? Easy—why didn't we say?
— Dan Crowe & Philip Oltermann

Vendela Vida
A Farewell to Arms

On my desk I keep a tattered copy of Hemingway's *A Farewell to Arms* because it's the book that made me want to be a liar and a writer.

The summer I was nine my family vacationed in Ketchum, Idaho. My Swedish mother, who wasn't a big reader but felt it was extremely important for my sister and me to read, took us on a bike ride to Hemingway's grave. First we had to pick a bouquet of flowers and then we had to figure out a way to carry the bouquets on our bikes without crushing them.

When we got to the grave there was a small crowd gathered around—two people taking a picture of the tombstone—and I felt a sense of excitement. The only graves I'd taken flowers to before were those of my grandparents and aunts. So I concluded I must be related to this man named Hemingway, and that being related to a man whose tombstone people took pictures of was a great honor. Finally, a famous relative!

It was a hot day and that afternoon, after the visit to the cemetery, I rode my bike with my friends, made a kite, and tried to catch a fish. I returned to the condominium where we were staying hopelessly sunburnt. My eyes stung from the sun, my clothing scratched my skin. My mother rubbed aloe cream on my shoulders and my back and I applied it to my face.

I couldn't move without something hurting, so I sat in front of the TV, wrapped in the soothing surface of a damp towel, determined not to change positions until it was time for bed. That night, *A Farewell to Arms* was on TV. "It's by the man whose grave we visited today," my mother said. I sat down in front of the TV with the kind of anticipation I'd last felt on New Year's Eve when I'd been allowed to stay up and watch Dick Clark in Times Square. But halfway through the movie, I suddenly felt profoundly sad. I loved the woman in the film; I was rooting for the couple. But the title haunted me: *A Farewell to Arms…* someone, I decided, was going to get their arms cut off. I tried to imagine my life without arms—no bike rides, no kites, no fishing. I began to cry. The salt from my tears stung like a jellyfish. I cried from the pain of crying. My parents couldn't understand what was going on—I was sobbing so hard I couldn't speak.

I refused to move though and I protested when they tried to turn the TV off. After a commercial break, the announcer said, "And now for the conclusion of *A Farewell to Arms*," I laced my fingers over my eyes the way I did when the wicked witch appeared in *The Wizard of Oz*.

But the movie ended, and no arms were lost. I was relieved, and then perplexed. I had been manipulated into crying, deceived into thinking that something horrid was going to happen based on a title. Hemingway, I decided, was a tricky, tricky man. The next day, layered in sunscreen and cloaked in a hat, a long-sleeve shirt, and pants, I biked to the library and read *A Farewell to Arms* from cover to cover in the cool air-conditioned room while a loud librarian told everyone else to be quiet.

That night I wrote my first short story. Looking back I doubt I could have understood everything that happened in *A Farewell to Arms*, but that wasn't the point. The point was that I wanted to deceive people, to keep them guessing, to make them care about a character so much that they would sob —or laugh—and never be able to guess the ending.

Jonathan Franzen
A Squeaky Office Chair

This is my office chair, which I've been using continuously since scavenging it off a street in Rockland County, New York, in 1982. It squeaks horribly and irremediably, but it's been many years since I've been able to hear the squeak, just as I can't hear myself talking when I write dialogue, even though, when I leave the office, I can tell from my hoarseness that I've been talking loudly all day.

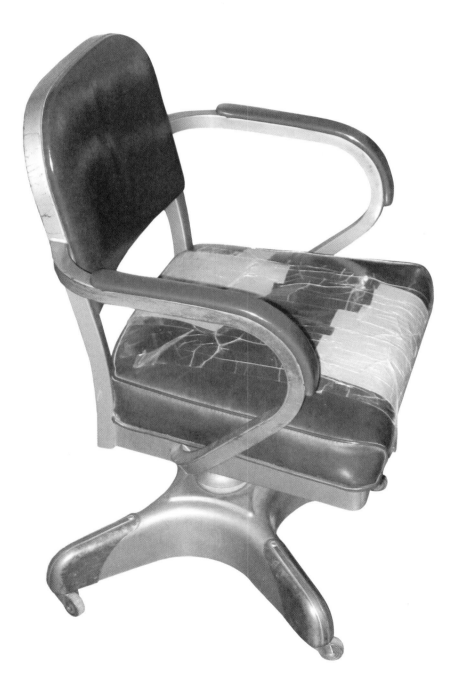

Will Self
Post-it Notes

I write ideas, tropes, images, observations, snippets
of dialogue, themes, factoids, descriptions on these Post-it
notes and put them in relevant zones on the wall. Then I
organize them into scrapbooks, then I turn them into books.
Then I write more ideas, etc., on Post-it notes. And so
it goes on: the auto-cannibalization of the fictive world.
All creative artists fetishize their working methods—but
it isn't ever nice to look at. At least I don't think so.

Alan Hollinghurst
The Baths of Diocletian

In the little study where I write I have a large Piranesi engraving of the ruins of the Baths of Diocletian in Rome, done, I think, in the 1750s. I bought it for myself as a present when my second novel came out 12 years ago.

It is one of Piranesi's diagonals, where a very long subject is shown in a very steep perspective. In the left of the picture the ruins block out the sky, and we seem to stand at the foot of towering walls—walls which, on the right-hand side, stretch away, dwindling and tree-tufted, to an immeasurable, and certainly exaggerated, distance. In Piranesi the scientific mind of the archaeologist was combined with the eye of a visionary poet. Close up, he shows us the construction of a huge functional building, brick, stone, and Roman concrete, each brick distinct and countable; but overall the impression is one of romantic magnificence.

It's a picture rich with a sense of work, the immense labor of the ancient builders and the complementary labors of Piranesi himself, paying homage to the ancient world in his obsessive delineation of detail. As a slow, pen-and-ink, brick-by-brick kind of writer, I find it, when I look up, both sobering and reassuring. There's so much to get right in that rearing foreground, and the present page is such a small part of the long rhythmic perspective. The poetry is the not quite calculable thing that has to grow and bind and transform the picture once it's done.

Benjamin Markovits
Stövchen

I'm the second tallest writer my wife has ever climbed into bed with. There was a poet who used to get drunk with her parents, and stay the night. (His name is Kit; he is six foot eight; he still gets drunk with them.) Kit slept in the attic, and Caroline, when she was a girl, used to wake him up in the morning and make him read to her. Kit's poems are the kind that give pleasure. He writes, among more serious verses, jokes, limericks, spoofs, and parodies. A number of his lines have slipped into the family idiom; his poems are one of the things I married into. He was the first proper poet I had ever met. By proper, I mean: memorizing, memorable, amused, amusing, and published.

There's a very good though heavy-handed sonnet by Keats about a poet's life. It begins: "When I have fears that I may cease to be." In it, he worries about dying before he has written all the good things he was born to write, or stared his fill at "the night's starred face" or the "fair creature of an hour." Keats, in the end, consoles himself with the thought that love and fame don't matter much in the scale of things. His poem reminds me of something a high school teacher once said about the ballad-writer Kurt Tucholsky. Tucholsky died very young; luckily, my teacher remarked, he had already written all his great works.

Kit condensed Keats's sonnet into something more cheerful, which brings me at last to the little stove in the photograph: or "stövchen," as my German mother calls it. "When I have fears that I may cease to be," Kit wrote, "I pour myself a second cup of tea." The first is the one you drink at breakfast. The second is what you take up to work: a warm defense against the blankness of the screen.

The candle at the bottom of it is hot enough to keep a hot drink hot from ten o'clock till lunch time, the most important hours of a day. It relieves, a little, the pressure to write; at least, that part of the urgency produced by the rate of cooling tea.

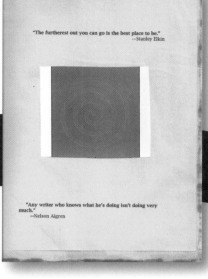

"The furtherest out you can go is the best place to be."
—Stanley Elkin

"Any writer who knows what he's doing isn't doing very much."
—Nelson Algren

Tom Robbins
Jarry's Spiral

For years, a homemade poster has hung above my writing desk. I suppose I made it to serve both as a reminder of certain important truths and as a kind of greeting, like the inscription on the Statue of Liberty, welcoming the nervous exile into a strange new land (in my case, the land of fictive prose that I've entered each morning as if for the first time).

The poster, if it can be called that, contains two quotations from writers and an image of a particular spiral. I say "particular" because this spiral, drawn allegedly by Alfred Jarry to decorate the bulbous belly of the title character of his infamous 1896 play, *Ubu Roi*, has long served as the symbol or logo for the (mostly) French avant garde movement (or anti-movement) known as 'pataphysics.

To define 'pataphysics for the uninitiated is challenging if not impossible. In fact, each 'pataphysician seems to have his own personal definition. My favorite claims 'pataphysics to be "the science of imaginary solutions." Let's just say that it's like a combination of Dada and Zen, with overtones of hallucinogenic poetics, resolute hedonism, and serious theoretical physics.

I should make it clear that I have no ambition whatsoever to compose 'pataphysical novels. Such an enterprise would reek of the deliberately esoteric. Nevertheless, to contemplate Jarry's insignia is persistently liberating because it reminds me that the frontiers of literary possibility extend far, far beyond the narrow perimeters imposed upon us in school.

Moreover, the spiral in and of itself is the fundamental shape of nature, of Everything. The Milky Way has spirality, as does our DNA. The crown of a daisy is a perfect logarithmic helix, and, more erratically perhaps, so is history, so are our lives. Looking each day at the spiral above my desk has prompted me to pay attention in my work to both the microcosmic and the macrocosmic, and has prevented me from succumbing (like so many of my peers) to the fraudulent notion that reality is intrinsically linear.

As for the two quotations, well, the words of Stanley Elkin are sort of a literary application of Einstein's advice to all creative thinkers: "Go out as far as you can go and start from there." It's hard advice to follow, difficult as hell, but it encourages you to be adventurous, to take risks, to chew on something larger and stranger than the old sociological meatball.

Nelson Algren, quite possibly the greatest North American writer of the 20th century, was wise enough to recognize that the best writing, the writing that really matters, arises not from an academic, analytical approach, but rather from a kind of *innocence*. Armed with all the imagination, wit, and heart you can muster, you follow the Charmer's pipes into the dark forest, naively confident that sooner or later, should you survive, you'll be led to those places where treasure is buried. To do it differently, to begin with a carefully calculated outline, for example, is to become little more than a manufacturer.

Janine Di Giovanni
A Maglite

In Sarajevo in 1992 I found my lucky charm.
It's a torch, a Maglite actually, which is ironic
because it was invented by a Croat and there
I was in the former Yugoslavia as the Croats
and Serbs were tearing the Muslims apart.

I found the torch on the seventh floor of the Holiday Inn. The Holiday Inn was an extraordinary place where all the journalists lived because it was the only game in town. How it ever operated is a great mystery and a testament to the black market. Situated on Sniper's Alley, it was a shell of a place, with no electricity, no water, and no heat. Because it was cavernous and Eastern Bloc–style architecture, it was absolutely freezing.

Our food came from the black market, rice and a kind of dog meat, but no one complained because we ate better than the civilian population who were selling their books and jewelry to buy bread. Because we were on Sniper's Alley, we got shelled and sniped out when we walked out the door. No one used an entire side of the building because it faced the hill where the Serb snipers lay in wait.

What was I doing wandering around the seventh floor of the Holiday Inn, you might ask? First of all, I can be forgiven for some naivety as it was my first real war, my first siege. I had reported misery before, and conflict, but this was the first time I knew some jerk was examining my window—or rather the plastic sheet that covered my window, the glass had been blown out long ago—through a sniper rifle. At night, I would lie fully clothed in four layers of clothing in my sleeping bag with the newfound Maglite reading Rebecca West and watching tracer rounds. I was lonely and frightened but I have to admit I felt a strange surge of excitement. Nothing like that had ever happened to me before.

I walked up the stairs to the seventh floor because I had never gone beyond the fifth, and all my life I have been too curious for my own good. There were rumors that Bosnian Muslim snipers were posted there, and I even had a girlfriend who said one sniper came down and had a cup of tea with her now and then (the water boiled off the generator in the Reuters office which had one of the few satellite phones in the building—50 dollars a minute).

I walked up alone. Past the fifth floor, it got mighty creepy. The wind whished through the holes in the building and I began to think this might not be such a great idea. But since I started, I was determined to finish. It was Christmas week, and most of the other journalists had gone home, and I had already filed my report for the week and I was a little bored, I have to admit.

I finally got there. The seventh floor was a total wreck. The carpet was chewed up. The windows were totally blown out. Rain and snow had seeped in, making the floors sag. Toilets were tossed in hallways, like strange orphans. There was a terrible smell of stale food, stale clothes, maybe stale flesh. Who knew?

Then I saw the Maglite on the ground, a little jewel in the midst of hell. I snatched it up and stared at it hard, then turned it on and off. It still worked, glowing faintly. I was about to turn and rush off with my prize when I looked up and saw a Bosnian soldier glaring at me. I smiled shyly, but he did not smile back. My romantic image of the sniper defending all of us in the Holiday Inn rapidly faded: he was just an exhausted soldier who had seen too much and had been staring through a sniper rifle for far too long. His eyes were reddened, and he was angry.

"Get the fuck out of here," he said in Bosnian. "Don't ever come back." I know he said this, because I ran downstairs to one of the interpreters in the Reuters office and carefully remembered most of his words and asked what it meant.

I realized on my way down the stairs that I still had the torch in my hand. He did not ask for it back—perhaps it was not his.

Over the next decade, that torch went everywhere with me, and my best writing went with it. To Grozny, Chechnya, when the city fell to Russian forces in February 2000. To Sierra Leone, where two friends, journalists, were murdered and I got surrounded by stoned teenage soldiers who wanted to rape me. To the Ivory Coast, where I woke up with a coup d'état in my garden. To Liberia, Rwanda, Somalia, East Timor, Vietnam, Serbia, Afghanistan, Iraq, Lebanon, Gaza, the West Bank, and Kosovo—where my KLA unit got bombed—and Montenegro, where I accidentally crossed the border into Kosovo and got captured, briefly, by paramilitary soldiers and marched into the woods with a gun pointing at my head. And also to Positano and Paris, where I finished my book, and Zimbabwe and a million other places.

I like to think it's simple luck that I am still here, but there are certain photographers who won't travel with me unless I bring the Maglite. I don't like to attribute too many powers to an inanimate object—I am a Catholic after all—but fourteen years on, it still has the piece of duct tape on it. And I am still here.

Eric Chase Anderson
A Cork Wall

I buy supplies from a library-supply company out in Wisconsin. They sell everything you need to run your own library—one-armed desks, Mylar bookjackets, lending-card pockets, and huge pieces of replacement cork. I tend to pin everything up so I can see it, and I thought an extra-large bulletin board would do the trick.

It came rolled up like wallpaper, soft and heavy. It was meant to be glued into some kind of frame —four feet by six feet. I didn't have a frame, so I mounted it right on the naked wall of my apartment here in New York, using the kind of tiny nails which are referred to as tacks. It took about twenty tacks.

It was winter when the cork arrived, and the cork laid down flat. When the spring rain came, the cork bubbled, and I had to use the rest of the tacks—over a hundred—to tamp it down again.

There are all sorts of objects on my cork wall, attached by pins and rubber bands.

There is a map of my stepmother's minivan, which I made as a Christmas present for my sister, an early, full-color prototype of a business card for my brother's film company, photographs of various models for characters (Steve McQueen for Uncle Gus, Maureen O'Hara for Mrs. Dugan, Bobby Driscoll for young Chuck), the bumblebee patch from Max's blazer in the movie *Rushmore*, a book called *Butterflies in Britain* by Richard Chopping, who did the dustjackets for the original James Bond novels, a Charles Adams cartoon from *The New Yorker* showing a little kid dressed up as a sailor, down to the tattoo of a naked lady on his chest, a photo of Roald Dahl and his famous writing shed, and a tiny copy of *Don Winslow of the Navy and the Giant Girl Spy*.

Then we have Corporal Dashiell Hammett (he's in the Army in the photo, smoking a cigarette in Alaska), Charles M. Schulz, Harper Lee, Jack London, Stephen Crane, Ian Fleming, Edgar Rice Burroughs, Robert Louis Stevenson, and a Norman Rockwell advertisement for Underwood Typewriters showing a boy writing at his desk, with a dreamy picture of a frontiersman hefting his long rifle above the legend: "… And Daniel Boone came to life on the Underwood portable."

Kiehl's LIP BALM #1

Contains soothing ingredients and moisturizing oils to provide relief to dry, chapped lips. Apply liberally, and allow an excess of the balm to be absorbed.

Kiehl's Since 1851, Inc.®
New York, NY 10003
For further information,
please call 1-800-KIEHLS-1
(1-800-543-4571)

net wt. 0.5 oz. (14 g)

413-1/2

JT LeRoy
Kiehl's

They all got it in their bathrooms. All the rich folks. Creak open their mirrored cabinet above the sink which got a joy stick dead center 'stead of knobs. I stealth pop vials, tubes, containers up my sleeve. This is special stuff, and it will adjust whatever is going to take place in their bed. What they've paid me for. They don't care about me. They don't care about me after... even if they say they do, I know they are still gonna want me to leave. But I will take some of this with me.

Man, they got some secret fucking club. Kiehl's, it's called. You never see adverts for it. They are too secret for that. You want it, you gotta be in the know. All these folks, they are in the know. They got Kiehl's vials, tubes, containers filled with crèmes, jellies, special glazes, soaps that don't stink of disinfectant. Boring white packaging, like they really are trying to keep it to their private circle. It reminds me of those Masonic orders I've read about. I pour "ABYSSINE SERUM" thick like yogurt into my left pocket, and "Baby Gentle Cleansing Milk" into my right. In the back pocket I stow ten valium, twenty vicodin, anything else that looks removing. My tricks, some of them, they care about themselves, these folks. They use rubbers, dental dams, bleach. They pay attention to dark splotches under their eyes. They care about things that make them need to find a place like Kiehl's that puts avocado in their crème. I hide a tube in my sock.

I take my first royalty check from my first sold book. I go into the Kiehl's store. Before, with my sponsor, I committed, "I ain't gonna steal, no matter how easy they make it. I ain't gonna nab nothin." I pace back and forth, nodding at the familiar vials, tubes, containers, like I was a lawyer listening to possible arguments. I glower at eye contact attempts from the staff—they're clad in these white lab coats—their outfits make me more at ease somehow. Like they're being honest about what they're selling—soothing anesthetic for me. "What ya like what ya need what can I do for you?" They don't say, they say something more genteel. Like I belong there. I mumble maybe my skin is a bit dry. But then it's like they pulled the magic string. The woman in the white lab coat sounded a little too concerned. Like she cared or something. And I can't shut up— "My lips are too cracked. I don't care about wrinkles, but maybe I should. I think I should. Should I care about wrinkles? I want to care about wrinkles. I have a bed to sleep in now—it is my own. I don't worry about that anymore. Wrinkles—that I am worried about. My lips have sores. That bothers me. I don't have lice though." They beam at me, maybe they are encouraged that I don't have lice, and they go to their wood drawers, and they rummage and they squeeze out tubes all from behind their counter. I step up onto my tippy-toes to watch them

in their preparations. Like watching at the zoo when the zookeeper is making the feed for the animals. I love how they mixed it in front of us, how the lions paced faster. I am salivating. The white coat lady hands me packets and mini plastic jars filled with magical serums to help with my new concerns. I shove all their free samples into my pockets. It is pleasant not to have wet mushy pockets. I nod my thanks. But I keep my word—I buy a five dollar lip balm. I use it every fifteen minutes. I paid for it. I showed my sponsor my receipt. There is a jar of those lip balms placed out on the counter, like door-prices, but I pay. Like they are just begging you to stick your hand in it and go right ahead please and take home a few, for free. I don't feel too stupid for not doing that. I actually feel proud palming my purchased lip balm. Just like the one I've seen in them rich folks' houses.

I am going to write. I am gonna take a hot-as-I-can-tolerate-it shower, like the kind that steams up the mirror and you can leave a secret message for the next person that bathes. I write it with my index finger. I get out, I combine every crème and jelly and serum and vial and tube and paste that has that Kiehl's name on it. That I am in on. My parchedness is bread to its gravy. I admire their dull packaging, I bought a lot of it. I didn't steal any of it from anyone's house or the Kiehl's store. Some they gave me to try. I didn't appropriate it. My fingertip is wet as the message I wrote in the mirror fog lifts away. Someone else will find it and laugh. It's a private joke. You don't take time to put crème on when you are in a group home or on the street or in a hospital. You gotta get out, another's turn. Next one. Plus, they take that stuff away. And the ones they give you reek bad, coat you like lard. I got a mug of hot green tea, a big bar of very dark chocolate. I am basked in my Kiehl's. I am in my pajamas. I am ready to write now. I am ready to go in. For the first cut.

Alain de Botton
A Large Desk

It's often said that the greatest thing about being a writer is that one is able to work anywhere. Why not do a book in Italy? Why not write a chapter in Marrakech? Yet this invitation to vagabondage skates over a critical dark feature of writing: the fear that one will never be able to write again, that one won't be able to re-create the ingredients that inspire writing in just any old hotel room, that one is not wholly in command of what one is doing and hence needs to root oneself to whatever spot was conducive to a previous successful effort. Therefore, whatever my putative freedom, for the last decade, I haven't dared to leave my city, even my home, for more than a few days, lest I wander too far from my desk: a sacred plinth of creativity.

The most notable feature of the desk is its size. It runs from one end of the room to the other, a good five meters of solid Canadian oak. Size is key because it enables me to spread an awe-inspiring number of books and pieces of paper all around me without generating a feeling of chaos. The desk is an instrument of order, a quality that is more important to me than any other when trying to write, not because I am an ordered person, but precisely because I constantly feel so close to anarchy. A book is in essence a giant exercise in order: an attempt to place some 80,000 pieces of jigsaw into a coherent and meaningful chain. But how to carry out this feat of logic without inspiration from the surrounding environment, without the lesson in order reinforced by the furnishings of the writer's room?

In part, the desk is an attempt to compensate for years when all the desks I worked on were too small. I remember years at university when books were constantly dropping off the edge of a spitefully small table. When I was finally in a position to buy a house and decorate my room as I wanted it to be, I behaved like a sheikh who has suddenly hit oil in the desert sands: I wasn't afraid to be vulgar. I enjoyed the surprise on the face of my carpenter, who told me repeatedly that I would live to regret my grandiose decision.

Ultimately, my dependence on my desk can be traced back to a troubling feature of my psychology: to the wilful, erratic nature of my creative self. This timid creature is absurdly easily disturbed, by a draught, a noise (any kind of clicking or low-level hissing sound), or even the wrong quality of light. There are always any number of excuses that arise for why it would be a better idea to sleep than to write. In this fragile state, I depend on my surroundings to assist the nobler sides of myself in their battle with their profane counterparts. It is as a vital part of this daily battle that I've come to rely on my desk. It promises me that whatever book I am working on could, whatever its current chaos, one day end up as ordered, calm, and expansive as the desk already is.

Luis J. Rodriguez
Ganesha

On my desk is a reclining Ganesha, the Hindu Lord of Success, the elephant-headed deity that oversees austere beginnings and the removal of obstacles. He is also believed to be the author of the Mahabharata, one of Hindu's major works, and as such a protector of writers.

As a writer, finding inspiration, a muse, a deity, or energy source, is not much appreciated in the general culture—although writers find them all the time. I look upon this rotund figure—Ganesha is round, like me—lying on its side, as if in contemplation, and I think about where writing comes from, the deep and often choppy ocean all writers swim in, draw from, and dwell. The statue's brown metal skin connects to my indigenous Chicano skin. And even if I'm not Hindu, I can immerse myself in its myriad images, symbols, and stories.

This particular statue was given to me last year by my friend, the mythologist and storyteller Michael Meade, on the occasion of the publication of my first novel, *Music of the Mill*. In the more than ten years I've worked with Michael Meade and other storytellers, healers, poets, and shamans, I've learned to seek vital ideas, languages, and typologies to orient my efforts to help troubled youth, in mentoring projects, and in my writing, publishing, and teaching.

Ganesha, at various times, can be found riding a mouse, with a serpent at its belly, or holding a book, a hatchet, a noose, or a gourd. He is also the God of education, knowledge, wisdom, and wealth. Because of his honored place in the Hindu pantheon, he is also slayer of vanity and selfishness, and is both the beginning and the meeting ground.

Having such a powerful entity grace my desk is an acknowledgment of my lifelong striving for deep knowledge, intense conscious awareness, and the responsibility of using words and language to teach, heal, overcome, and shape. My work is informed with the basic motive impulses that have driven most social movements in this country and the world—real justice, true equity, and the full and healthy development of everyone.

A healthy and balanced earth (abundant, protected, understood, and replenished) and a healthy and balanced society (with its core interests and objectives tied to the well-being of all humans and other life) are my key concerns. This is where I place most of the focus and drive of my poems, my short stories, my children's books, my books and essays.

Although my particular spiritual path is based on Native American and Native Mexican traditions, I am open to learn from all spiritual expressions, religious practices, and cultural/social traditions. They all contain truth and validity in them, even though not one of them is true or valid for everybody. My writing, which is my life, not just my job, has a spiritual and soul-rooted foundation. Thus the importance of Ganesha on my desk near my computer, energizing all projects with the fire-source of wisdom and good results.

Gina Ochsner
A Picture from Prague

A pack rat at heart, I've never been able to escape the pull of objects, of collecting. Next to the phone (circa 1940s and completely nonfunctional) a thick white shell rests on its back and in the smooth hollow, gifts from my six-year-old son: a sprig of dried hyssop and feather from a downed crow. From a distance the filaments of the feather appear glossy black, but when examined under the hand-held glass, they deepen to an inky blue. On top of the computer a hula figurine sways her grass-skirted hips beside a rolling metal replica of a Soviet Aeroflot passenger plane. My Russian neighbor insists the name of the airline is not, repeat *not*, onomatopoetic.

On the days when I need a little extra kick in the pants to keep going I look to Nunzilla: the Fire-Breathing Nun. A few turns of the spring, and sparks shoot from her mouth, and in one arm, she wields a ruler. Balancing on the carriage of an old Soundless Typewriter is the latest of my shelved experiments: a dish of white capped mushrooms with magenta gills. According to my mushroom encyclopedia, this particular fungus is either one of the most highly sought-after on account of its choice culinary quality, or it is one of the most poisonous mushrooms known to man. One of these days, I'll muster up my courage and find out for sure which it is.

I love these objects—each of them a treasure for different reasons. Each of them carries a small story, a reminder of a journey or a person I love and who is gone now, or of something I want to know more about. But of all the items I've collected, the one that always gives me pause is a picture mounted above the mushrooms, above the Soundless. This picture came from a tiny shop on Celetna Street in the old Hradcany district of downtown Prague. What first struck me was how vibrant the colors are and the way the sky bleeds in warmth and gentleness. And though I can't hear the violin's music, I imagine that the sound of the bow over the bridge gives the angels their wings. And I wonder if the man in the painting, whose eyes are closed, even knows how this invisible music creates levity, flight, buoyancy, and even joy.

Every morning I look at this picture and I never stop feeling grateful and humbled and astonished at how another artist's vision and imagination transports me, daily reminding me of the kind of artist I want to be: carried on the invisible back of something larger, beautiful, buoyant, and far wiser than myself.

Douglas Coupland
Chocolate

Last summer I had some stomach problems and had to remove several items from my diet—chocolate, hard liquor, and tomatoey foods. Around that same time began a period of writer's block that, after seven months or so, began to frighten me. I think all writers are superstitious that way—that somehow, someday, whatever it is that makes their voice their own will simply leave. When you're inside writer's block it's horrible because you're simply not *you* anymore. You're this person who *used* to be you. Now you're this person who's going to have to get a day job. This winter I also began going to the gym with a trainer five days a week, and after a few weeks I noticed that in general, when exercising, it takes my endorphins about 45 minutes to kick in. I've never been a jock, and I always thought endorphins were a media hoax, but they do exist, and once your system releases them exercise becomes (and this is something I'd never ever be writing) *fun*.

I asked my trainer, Neil, how long it takes his endorphins to kick in, and he said maybe five minutes—so I began to wonder if maybe there's one simple chemical reason for jocks being jocks and nerds, nerds: endorphin release rate. I asked Neil if he could find out if there was a food or a pill I could eat before the gym to speed up endorphin release. His answer? Chocolate.

So I began eating dark chocolate two hours before working out and was shocked at the almost instant change in my body's response to activity—I loved it—my happy chemicals were releasing within five minutes. I was wary of a placebo effect, but it's been a month now, and my endorphins kick in, bingo, right on the five-minute mark.

But the big shocker was that my writers' block ended! This was a block so bad that in its midst, writing even these simple few hundred words could never have happened. And I owe it to chocolate: specifically Baker's milk chocolate chips, which come in 300g bags—the chips used in chocolate chip cookies. Without these chips, there is no work. It's that binary. I keep them to the left of my keyboard and I eat maybe fifty or so medicinally once a day.

The one sad thing that happened as a result of this is that I no longer enjoy the taste of chocolate—my brain has reclassified it as a medicine, and frankly, I wish I could take chocolate pills and not have to taste it anymore. Nature is, if nothing else, perverse.

Melissa Bank
A Blindfolded Rhino Rescued from Floodwaters

I came upon this picture in the *New York Times* after I'd published my first book and was trying to write my second.

Publication is what every unpublished writer I've ever met wants and hopes for and it's what I'd wanted and hoped for, and yet it had its difficulties. For one thing, it made me aware of writing as a public act, as I never had before.

The next time out, I wanted to be in control. The only problem: for me to write anything worth reading I can't be in control. My conscious mind, the part that cares what critics might hate or readers might like, has to get out of the way for me to get anything done. My subconscious does all the heavy lifting, which brings me back to this picture.

It's tacked above the writing table at my cabin to remind me of how writing really works. I don't mean that it's a precise metaphor; it's more like an image from a dream about writing. It captures the emotion for me—the ungainly struggle, the possibility of rescue, the blind faith writing requires. It also reminds me that the alternative is drowning in a flooded cage in the zoo.

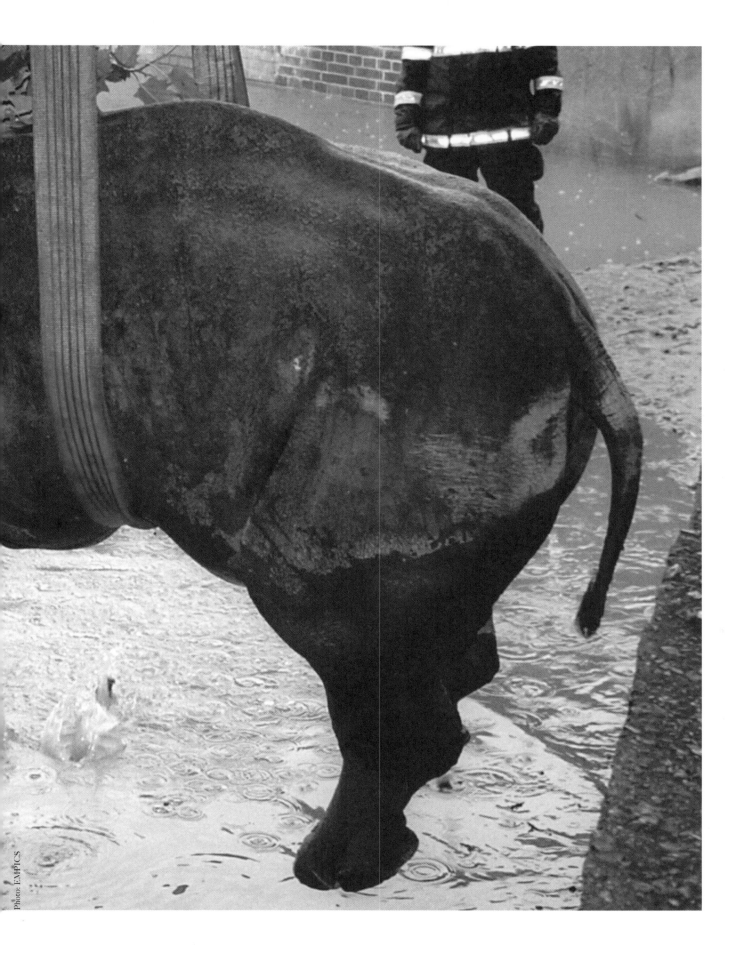

David Baddiel
Simon Wiesenthal and the Simpsons

For the last couple of years, I have written in a study overlooking water. This may be psychologically helpful in many ways, but for the purposes of this piece I'm choosing to see it mainly as a conduit between the two pictures that hang on opposing walls around my desk. On my right, a signed photograph of Simon Wiesenthal; on the other, a framed montage of four *TV Guides* depicting a mural—a polyptych, I believe, is the word—of the Simpsons at home. Every time I look up from my work, I am being stared at either by the world's greatest Nazi hunter or by Bart with a cartoon remote control. I cannot imagine a narrative or psychological issue that might come up whilst writing which would not be on the spectrum thus created between them. That, and the pond outside, allow me to feel that I am genuinely covering the creative waterfront.

Lionel Shriver
Clippity

This is Clippity. He reminds me to eschew fancy-schmancy character names groaning from overloads of symbolism, and to sometimes prefer the obvious. As a child I had a taste for simplicity, to which in mature decrepitude I return.

Clippity keeps me humble. Along with a little glass-framed photo atop my two-volume OED—a shot of me at two years old, sporting jaggedly cut blonde bangs, patting a stuffed rabbit, and ogling into the camera with a trusting expression that I pray I have never worn since—Clippity recalls my modest origins. He is a totem of the truism that at its best fiction is play, and a stern admonishment that taking "my work" (how is it that such a straightforward formulation has come to sound so pretentious?) too seriously is a sure route to writing the very ponderous, killjoy tomes that I cannot bear to read myself.

Incredibly, Clippity still works. On uninspired afternoons (and they are legion), I can wind up my tenacious toy, and he will clop-clop-clop across the wood. If a cheap threadbare donkey from Howard Johnson's can walk the walk after over forty years, surely my rusty imagination can crank out another miserable paragraph at an age barely more advanced.

I am a wordy writer, and often churn out pages on end without advancing the plot a jot. Hence I try to take my cue from a childhood impatience with any device that doesn't get somewhere. Even in his sprightly youth, Clippity had a problem with running in place—just like my first drafts—when the surface was too slick. As a kid, I was ingenious enough to smear green Plasticine on his rear hooves. Thus I discovered the importance of traction, as handy a concept in literature as for wind-up toys.

Note that in this photo Clippity is led by a tiny clay "penitent," which a friend brought me from Spain. That figure in the peaked purple hood somehow manages to convey both an intrepid fearlessness and a respect for mystery and magic. It is in precisely such a twin spirit that I venture into every new novel. Having the nerve to write yet another book in a world already drowning in blather requires bravery, arrogance, and willful naiveté; at once, you have to concede that when a novel clicks (*clippity-clippity*), some alchemy has been achieved of which you are not entirely the master.

As for the concept of "penitence," this cloaked shaman—who looks a little like an unusually colorful member of the Ku Klux Klan—emblemizes the fact that, for every time I craft a crap sentence, grind out a boring or grossly gratuitous passage (without traction), or take a turn in my plot so obvious that my readers could have come up with it themselves so what do they need me for, I am *very, very sorry*.

Geoff Dyer
Through My Window

Over the years I have come across several places that offered the ideal conditions in which to work. The room in Montepulciano, for example, with the lovely wooden bed and white sheets, the window gazing out over the Tuscan countryside, the terrace formed by what had once been a little bridge connecting our building to the one next door. Or the house in Lauzun with the room overlooking a field of wheat, facing west so that in the evenings the paper on the desk was bathed red.

Or my apartment on rue Popincourt with the floor-to-ceiling window from which you could see right down rue de la Roquette, as far as the Bastille almost.

What they all had in common, these ideal places for working, was that I never got any work done in them. I would sit down at my desk and think to myself what perfect conditions for working, then I would look out at the sun smouldering over the wheat, or at the trees gathering the Tuscan light around themselves, or at the Parisians walking through the twilight and traffic of rue de la Roquette, and I would write a few lines like "If I look up from my desk I can see the sun smouldering over the wheat"; or "Through my window: crowded twilight on the rue de la Roquette"; and then, in order to make sure that what I was writing was capturing exactly the moment and mood, I would look up again at the sun smouldering over the flame-red wheat or the crowds moving through the neon twilight of rue de la Roquette and add a few more words like "flame-red" or "neon," and then, in order to give myself over totally to the scene, would lay down my pen and simply gaze out at the scene, thinking that it was actually a waste to sit here writing when I could be looking and by looking–especially on rue de la Roquette where the pedestrians hurrying home in the neon twilight would look up and see a figure at his desk, bathed in the yellow light of the angle-poise–actually become a part of the scene whereas writing involved not an immersion in the actual scene but its opposite, a detachment from it. After a very short time I would grow bored by contemplating the scene, would leave my desk and go for a walk in the wheatfield sunset or leave my apartment and walk down to the Bastille so that I could become one of the people walking back through the neon twilight of the rue de la Roquette, looking up at the empty desk, bathed in the light of the angle-poise...

When I thought of the ideal conditions for working, in other words, I looked at things from the perspective of someone not working, of someone on holiday, of a tourist in Taormina. I always had in mind the view that my desk would overlook, thereby overlooking the fact that the view from the desk is invisible when you are actually working, and forgetting that of the many genres of sentence I dislike there is none that I despise more than ones which proceed along the lines of "If I look up from my desk..." The ideal conditions for working were actually the worst possible conditions for working.

And in any case maybe all this fuss about the conditions for working was irrelevant. After all, did it matter so much where you lived? The important thing, surely, was to find some little niche where you could work; to settle into a groove and get your work done. Logically, yes, but once, in north London, I had found myself walking along the road where Julian Barnes lived. I didn't see him but I knew that in one of these large, comfortable houses, Julian Barnes was sitting at his desk, working, as he did every day. It seemed an intolerable waste of a life, of a writer's life especially, to sit at a desk in this nice, dull street in north London. It seemed, curiously, a betrayal of the idea of the writer. It made me think of a picture of Lawrence, sitting by a tree in the blazing afternoon, surrounded by the sizzle of cicadas, notebook on his knees, writing: an image of the ideal condition of the writer.

Or so it had appeared in memory. When I actually dug it out it turned out that there was no notebook on his knees. Lawrence is not writing, he is just sitting there: which is why, presumably, it is such an idyllic image of the writer.

Anthony Bourdain

Nicotine

Other than a writing implement and paper, the single item essential to my writing career–indispensable to the very task of setting words to paper–is a pack of cigarettes. No smokes? No writing. However unhealthy or unlovely that equation–there it is. I can't do without them. I'm a morning writer, meaning that I'm at my best and smartest very first thing after I get up. As the day goes on, the slower and stupider and lazier I get. And the day–every day–begins with a cigarette. General routine on a good writing day is to wake up, light up, sit down and begin–then continue without interruption for as long as I can. If I break for a few minutes to, say … run out and buy cigarettes, the thing is lost. I smoke a lot when I write; which is to say constantly and unconsciously. I like to think I'm self-medicating. I am, probably, nicer and more attentive when smoking. I shudder to think what harm I might do to those I care about– and the world around me–without the calming, modulating effects of nicotine. I'll never quit. I've quit heroin. I've quit cocaine. In both cases, successfully beating considerable odds. I think I've done enough. I deserve to hang on to those few vices I have left–and unlike my other vices, I can smoke while writing. Only thing worse than no cigarette is a menthol cigarette. Can't write on no damn menthols. Can't live. In fact, faced with a future of only menthol cigarettes? I'd probably hang myself in the shower stall.

Siri Hustvedt
Unknown Keys

My father was a supremely organized man. After he died, my three sisters and I read through countless letters, papers, and documents he had filed, according to one lucidly explicated category or another, and then decided what to keep and what to discard. One day while I was working in the room alone, I came across a small green box. In it was a metal ring with seven keys of various sizes. Attached to the ring was a small chain with a label, on which my father had written in his unmistakable hand: "Unknown Keys." I now work with these unknown keys near me. They have become not only a reminder of my father—the man who is no longer there—but a sign of the act of writing itself. These keys to phantom doors, suitcases, safes, and diaries are linked in my mind to making stories. Now orphaned, they serve only as literal doubles of the imaginary keys that unlock nameless interiors: the peculiar dream spaces of fiction.

A.L. Kennedy
Notebooks Thrown
Across Rooms

Maybe it's my age, maybe it's my life—the thing is, I don't really have any little talisman or gimmick that's specifically intended to support my writing. I suspect that whatever calls in my words would frown on any simplification of our relationship, any reliance on the tangible. The closest I ever got to a support mechanism was the picture of someone I loved who seemed to understand the isolation and petty terror of the whole process and who seemed to care if I was putting one page after another and if I was comfortable in the meantime. But that didn't last long. And, to be honest, the picture was something of a distraction—given the choice, I generally preferred looking at him to staring at scribbled rewrites, or a bleak computer screen. Now I've fallen back down to my usual nothing—which certainly doesn't distract. It never did.

So I spend half the year alone in various hotel rooms, trying to climb out of my mind, and the other half sees me stuck in my study doing much the same. This, in itself, would probably shake loose even the most tenacious objects. As I have none, I needn't worry I'll misplace them. But I am left with one prop—the notebook.

Each book has a notebook—a kind of first home that scraps of it might be tempted to visit. The notebook must be small enough to fit in my pocket, big enough to accommodate drawings, screams, doubts, plans, journal entries, records of self-loathing, and fragments of whatever story I'm trying to invent. The notebook must be willing to go with me everywhere: to be wet, worn, dirty, and occasionally thrown across rooms. And, when held in the hand, it must provide the kind illusion that really it does contain everything—character, detail, plot—the whole book ready for me, just waiting to be copied out.

Now they're lucky if they get a thousand on a live racing day. Horse racing in Oregon is dying and has been since I moved there ten years ago from Reno, Nevada. Now Portland Meadows is a nearly empty building with large sections closed off to the public, and both jockeys and horses are at the end of their professional line.

I'd never been to a horse track until then, but it was one of the first things I did when I moved to Portland, and I fell in love with the place the first time I set foot inside. I couldn't believe my luck. The crazy old lonely men, the degenerate gamblers, the bar, the cowboys, the Mexican ranchers, and the semi-pro handicappers. I began going three times a week. They have tables on the second floor and I'd drink beer and try to work on stories in between races. For years I have done that. Now I dream about it when I'm not there, and when I hate the town and want to leave it for good, it's the track that often keeps me from moving.

Lately I've been going out there early in the morning. I bring a Thermos of coffee and sit on the main floor and try to write. Outside I can see the horses work out and down the way from me I can hear the handicappers yelling at the TV screens as they bet on tracks in Arizona and New York and California.

It's not the gambling or the idea of trying to develop a system that attracts me. It's the building and the horses and the fans and the jockeys and how it's all hanging on by a thread. I feel at home around that. I can write well in a place like that.

Every year there is talk circulating that the track is finished, that this year really is going to be the last. The handle's down, the corporation is going to sell the land to a mall developer, the state won't renew the licenses because of environmental concerns. I worry like hell when I hear that. It breaks my heart. I don't know what I'd do if it wasn't there. Would I have to move to Turf Paradise in Phoenix? Would it be the same? What if this is the only place I'll ever get in my life that makes me feel like that? It might seem foolish to put so much value on a worn-out track, but in the end I guess it's just lucky to have someplace to go where you feel all right about yourself. Where you fit in.

So I go out as much as I can and stumble through my stories and am grateful for the big empty building and the horses and the jockeys or even when I hear some old man yell at the TV or hear some middle-aged guy screaming at a horse who just lost him $500.

Louisa Young
Calaca

I'd been trying to turn my life into a country-and-western song and was doing quite well. I was staying in Los Angeles. We went to Mexico for the day: David, me, and Joe the Sicilian/German dentist. The Oldsmobile I'd driven from Nashville and just sold to Joe for £500 exploded in a lay-by outside San Diego (as far as I know it's still there).

We drank a lot on a roof and ate oysters with chili sauce and at the border I tried to give my passport to a woman with a lot of children. Time sort of melted and David and I thought we might get married but he couldn't find the wedding chapel. Or maybe that was the other time. Later something very bad happened that I can't talk about.

I saw her in a tourist shop in Tijuana, sitting there, working away, tiny and hunched and with mad hair. I liked her and I bought her. She cost two dollars. I got a guy playing the trumpet as well, to be my brother playing his trumpet, and a guy on a motorbike, all bones but with a crash helmet, to be my friend who had recently died in a bike crash. This was sixteen years ago. They sit on my mantelpiece. She's me.

Isabel Young
People I Don't Know

I call it collecting people. Their names are Sophia and Martin (in that order). I found them in the street near our house, and they've lived on our windowsill ever since. They help my imagination, because I like to make up stories of their lives and characters, often over breakfast, like when I used to write books with Mum. Their names used to change with each new story, but then they settled and stayed. I think they must be discarded passport photos, and I like the idea that they really look much better than in the pictures. I hope I'll find more one day.

Photo by Philip Grey

James Flint
Yerba Maté

Yerba maté is drink of the gods—
the Guarani gods who roam the hillsides
and forests of northern Argentina,
I grant you, but gods all the same.

I first came across the drink while traveling in Patagonia with a posse of gauchos. Every morning when they woke and after every meal—meals which tended to consist of little other than a large hunk of animal smelted over an open fire—they filled a gourd or cup with something that looked like dried horse manure, stuck a metal straw in the top, and filled it to the brim with hot water decanted from a grimy plastic thermos flask. Then they sucked on it and passed it on, like a peace pipe.

This was maté, and apparently it was important that I would take my turn on the thing if I wanted to be accepted by the group. I sipped cautiously, not least because they'd refused to properly boil the river water they were using to infuse it, and feigned enthusiasm. When they weren't looking, I made myself a cup of instant coffee instead.

Back in Buenos Aires, I soon discovered that the drink wasn't a quaint local custom but a national obsession enjoyed by urban sophisticates as well as rural hayseeds. Maté, friends explained, is Argentina's national drink, responsible for 53% of the infusions market (i.e. more than coffee and tea combined). The country produces 300,000 tons of yerba—the tea itself—every year. Entire supermarket shelves are filled with it, and you can buy matés—the drinking gourds—all over the place, from extravagant ornamental versions encrusted with silver caps and pedestals to homely, disposable wooden cups that cost a few pesos each.

Besides your maté and your yerba, you need two other pieces of kit to properly enjoy your brew: a special metal drinking straw, or *bombilla*, and a thermos flask. Water that's too hot burns the leaf (and your mouth); it's important that you heat it to around 70°, or until tiny bubbles start appearing in the bottom of the pan or kettle. As you're constantly refreshing the water in the gourd, and it may be some time before the yerba runs out of potency, a thermos flask helps you keep the water at the correct temperature for the duration of the drinking process.

All this hassle and paraphernalia is ideal for writers, of course, as it involves loads of time-wasting and general fucking about (vital for nurturing the creative impulse). But the drink also has an active ingredient, a xanthine called mateine that acts as a muscle relaxant while simultaneously stimulating the central nervous system. The result is a clear-headed high that is calm, smooth, and free from any of the irritation, habituation, and sleeplessness you get from drinking too much skinny latte. In other words, the perfect state of mind for prolonged intellectual endeavor.

Flex paraguariensis also happens to contain nearly all of the vitamins and minerals necessary to sustain life. It alleviates depression, combats insomnia, regulates the gastric system, lowers blood pressure, improves hair color, increases the supply of oxygen to the heart during exercise, and encourages longevity. It suppresses appetite and lowers cholesterol. It's quite common for the Guarani Indians, who first cultivated the plant, to remain hale and hearty through long periods of famine by drinking copious quantities of their favorite brew. Which gives the writer another estimable advantage—even if working on low budgets late into the night, you never have to send out for pizza.

Two years on from my gaucho experience I can't live without the stuff. I certainly can't write without it. Good thing it tastes like shit, or you'd all be drinking it.

1

Rick Moody
Oblique Strategies[1]

Thereabouts or 1979 in it about heard first. Thereabouts. Heard first. Already interested in chance procedures at that time. Already interested thereabouts. Already listening to Cage. Already. Liked Eno solo albums. Liked Music for Airports. Listened to Music for Airports almost every day. Liked repetitions. Put on Music for 18 Musicians at the college radio station. Went out for coffee. Read about Oblique Strategies in some article about Eno. Read about Oblique Strategies. Had been throwing I Ching because Cage and Cunningham did it. Did not know how to find a box of Oblique Strategies instructional cards. Big blank where procurement was concerned. How to find? Big blank.

[1]Oblique Strategies cards used to compose these lines: "Reverse," "Emphasize repetitions," "Would anybody want it?," "Disciplined self-indulgence," "Accretion," "Do the words need changing?," "Honor thy error as a hidden intention," "Don't be frightened of clichés," "Always first steps," "Is it finished?"

Don't be frightened of cliches

Be Dirty

Consider transitions

Are there other sections?

Honor thy error as a hidden intention

Thereabouts or 1979 in, find to hard, Strategies Oblique. Didn't care if the whole thing was a little too abstract. Didn't care if no one wanted what I was doing. Didn't care. Already listening to The Residents and Pere Ubu, or soon thereafter. Already listening to Throbbing Gristle. Didn't care. Procurement issues with Oblique Strategies, and yet Oblique Strategies had begun to assume legendary status in creative life, alongside vanished masterpieces like Frank Zappa's *Läther* and Bruno Schulz's lost novel, *The Messiah*. Assumed Oblique Strategies was out of price range. Maybe just lazy. Maybe just did what I wanted to do. Insufficiently industrious. Some years passed where the artist in question was no longer in heavy rotation. Stopped thinking about Eno obsessively. Years in which lazy. Years in which insufficiently industrious, as regards abstract experiments, which are useful to creative life. Suddenly, in middle-nineties, became interested again (briefly) in electronic music; suddenly, in middle-nineties, started listening to Eno; suddenly, in middle-nineties, after years of listening only to things with guitars, began (briefly) to accept synthesizers, electronics; suddenly, in prose writing, began experimenting relentlessly. Who was to tell me otherwise? Didn't care. Experimented. Maybe it can be put a different way, maybe it can be construed as a sudden consonance with youth, maybe it can be construed as an epiphany of acceptance with certain

Do the words need changing?

Remember those quiet evenings

Is there something missing?

Gardening, not architecture

strains of thinking from the past. Putting it the right way? Eno as stepping-stone in process of embracing modernism as a whole, from Zurich and Paris up through Ulysses, Faulkner, Gaddis, Pynchon, DeLillo, etc.? Programmatic approach to writing? What kind of program? The kind with less revision and more voice, the kind where work happens, disengaged from the perfect surface of American naturalist writing, mistakes are good, comma splices are good, first thought best thought, love it or leave it, if the shoe fits, a bird in the hand, a stitch in time, all's well that ends well, well ends that well all's. By motivated coincidence: became possible to purchase items such as Oblique Strategies on a certain web site where things were auctioned off, became incredibly important to procure a copy of Oblique Strategies, bidding in many auctions, losing in many auctions, always the bidders in the last minutes. Kept offering more and more money, bidding a rather absurd amount of money, finally won (!), well, it turned out it was a signed copy of Oblique Strategies, had not focused on details, probably shouldn't keep it on my desk, shouldn't use, because of Eno signature, fuck that, produce work, produce prose, produce repose, produce. Shameless promotional sentence: Now Oblique Strategies is being manufactured anew, and you can get them for all your friends. Have I as.

Remove ambiguities and convert to specifics

Jane Smiley
Hot Water

I wrote my first novel in 1972 (unpublished) in a one-room apartment on Crete, using a fragile Royal portable typewriter, dressed in a caftan I sewed from a bedspread. I am writing my current novel, in 2006, in a reclining chair, on a Mac iBook G4 placed on a rolling desk. The room, this room, happens to be filled with pictures of horses, which remind me of a lot of things, including bills. I have my ancient Penguin paperback Roget's and my Columbia Desk Encyclopedia from 1967, but actually, there is no object that has, over the years, remained iconic, or even meaningful to my writing life.

Photo by Ty Canning

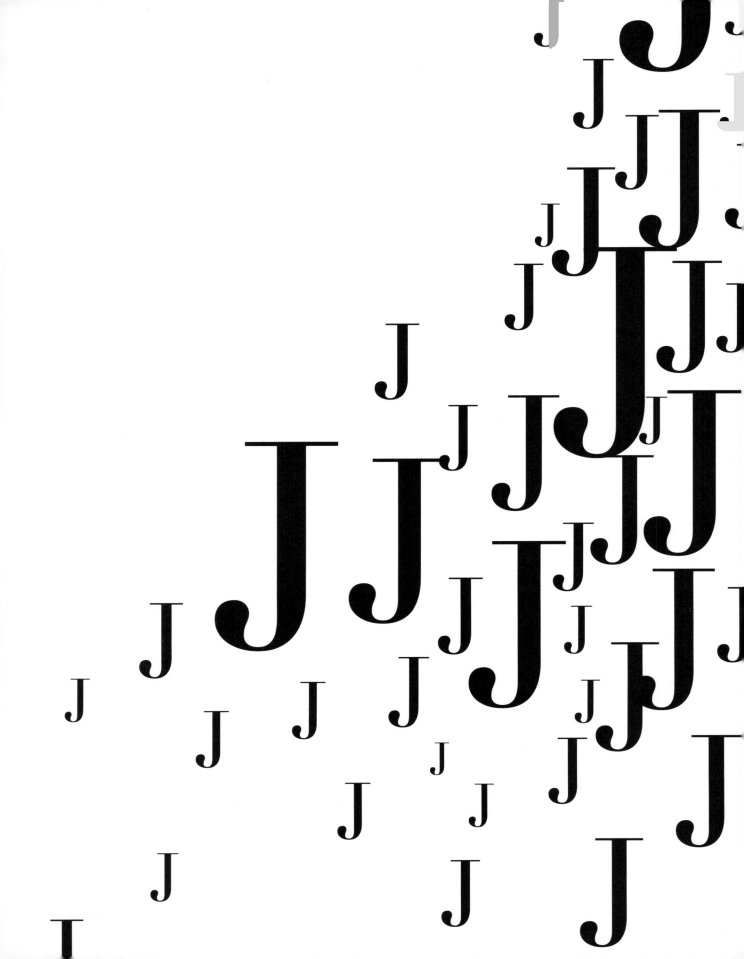

The locations, the motives, the furnishings, the equipment, the pictures on the walls, and the objects on the surfaces have all changed (though maybe the degree of clutter has endured). Nevertheless, when blocked, I have always had recourse to the same remedy—water. Bath, hot tub, or shower, it never fails. I sit, I think. I am stumped. I wish the phone would ring. I sigh. I go into the kitchen and rummage for something sweet. I find some old cookies or halvah. But no—when I sit down in my chair again, still blank. So I go into the bathroom and turn on the water.

I disrobe. I step in. It's hot, almost hotter than I can stand for about ten seconds. Within moments, I know what to write next. But I don't get out. As long as the water flows, I know I won't forget, so I stay in. Usually, I use up all the hot water in the tank. I wash my hair, soaping it and using conditioner. I cultivate my little thought, but really, I know it doesn't need anything more than the water can provide —now it needs fingers. I get out and dry off. By this time, I'm too impatient to put layers of clothes on, so I find my bathrobe (pink terrycloth Frette, from Costco) and my slippers (tan Merino, from the duty-free shop in Brisbane) and sit in my chair again. I don't know why the water did it in the beginning, but now it's just a conditioned response, I am sure. It could be worse and a lot more trouble— drinking, driving, fighting, shopping, something like that, but after all these years, it's only hot water.

Ian Rankin
Oxford Bar

The object in my office I treasure most is probably a framed photograph. It shows the battered signage above Edinburgh's Oxford Bar. The photo was taken by a guy called Andy Hall. He was putting together a book of photos of places chosen by Scottish celebrities. These places were to show something of the "spirit" of Scotland. Well, plenty of spirit gets knocked back inside the Oxford Bar, so I decided that I'd have the pub sign.

I've been drinking in the Oxford Bar since I was
a student in the 1980s (a fellow student—one of
my flat-mates—was part-time barman there). The
first time I walked in, I was a stranger. By my third
visit, my preferred drink was being poured before
I needed to ask. That's the "Ox" for you: it's like
a private club, only with no joining fee. It's also
a democratic place: everyone's as good as anyone
else, so long as they have the price of their next
drink about their person. There are few frills
to the Ox: no piped music, little in the way of hot
food (pies, pasties). It's a place for drink and for
conversation. I decided Inspector Rebus would
like it, so he started drinking there, too. (It helped
that back in the 1980s, the Ox was much favored
by the local constabulary!)

The Ox has been around for over a hundred
years, so it also represents tradition in an age
of change. And I always emerge from it with
something useful: a new joke; a line of dialogue;
a character trait or even an anecdote that can be
turned into a plot. It appeals to me also because
it's part and parcel of the "hidden city" that I try
to reveal to the world through my books. Though
sited in the city center, only a two-minute walk from
Princes Street's west end, the Ox lies up a narrow
alley, and gets little in the way of passing trade. It's
a secret corner of a busy urban environment, and
can sometimes seem like an oasis—though perhaps
not to the casual observer, who would see only its
nicotine-stained ceiling, caked with years of layered
gloss paint, and its rickety seating (pews taken from
a deconsecrated church). Look beyond the surface,
however, and you're in the real Edinburgh.

These days, however, the Ox gets a more varied
clientele than previously: Rebus fans from all over
the world make the pilgrimage, some of them part
of the official Rebus walking tour of the city. But
when they melt away, the bar takes on its old shape
and feel. Tiny as it is, it seems to contain multitudes.

That photograph helps me get inside the head
of Rebus, and of other characters in any Edinburgh-
based book I happen to be writing. It keeps me
grounded, and also acts as a taskmaster: if I can get
a good day's work done, I can reward myself with
a pint later on...

One mystery remains: on the signage, the word
"Oxford" is contained within inverted commas.
No one has been able to tell me why. Maybe it's
a case for Inspector Rebus.

A.S. Byatt
A Cabinet of Curiosities

The attic I write in is like a cabinet of curiosities—an idea that excited me the moment I met it. Or it is like Kipling's Kim's Game, a tray of objects to memorize. I collect glass paperweights and bits of rock—volcanic lava from Iceland, Phantom Quartz from Norway, Rose Quartz given to me by a Korean friend, a piece of chalky cliff from Flamborough Head in Yorkshire. I have a case full of brilliant South American insects—I'm not sure about the ecological propriety of these, but they were already dead and beautiful when I found them.

ANTONIA
WRITING TIME

The walls are lined with books, there is an inner bookcase surrounding my chair, and books are encroaching on the floor space in more or less orderly heaps. I write with a pen and have banished the computer to the other attic. I look out on treetops, and have herons and parakeets flying past my window (we have both in south London) and a family of foxes on the glass roof one floor down.

I chose my objects to represent my writing. The book and the Creature represent the sense I have that I write because there are imagined things very powerful in the world. *Asgard and the Gods* was my mother's crib for Ancient Norse and Icelandic at Cambridge—I read it again and again and again as a small child in the war. I find the Norse gods more exciting and mysterious (and powerful) than the Greek and Roman ones. I have been asked to write a modern version of any myth, and have chosen Ragnarok, the final death of all the gods.

The Creature I found in a junk shop in Sevenoaks when I was 18. I paid seven shillings and sixpence for him. He is very heavy, like a French boule, and his head takes off to make an inkwell—he must have held a pen in his hands. He has a strange tail curling up his back. I have no idea where he came from or when he was made but he clearly belongs to the world of northern tales of trolls and goblins. He has never had a name.

The third object is one of a series of notices Carmen Callil sent me when she was my publisher —a very long time ago. It represents any writer's endless problem—the temptation and imperative, alternately, of doing things that are not writing. Writing can, unfortunately, always be put off. The notices really work, and stop me distracting myself.

Adam Thirlwell
Laurence Sterne

I'm not much given to hero-worship, but I am faithful to my rare idolizations. One of these idols is Laurence Sterne. I mainly love him for his prose. But I also love him for his face—and, in particular, his face in its portrait by Joshua Reynolds, with its dramatic cheekiness, the ironic point of his pointed nose. And so, in the form of a postcard, I put him up above the table where I work as a kind of comic souvenir. I'm not sure how long he'll stay there, but I like him in front of me for now. His postcard gives me a sense of proportion. It's difficult, when writing underneath that ghosted smile, to walk the line of gravity. Comedy seems more serious instead.

Photo by Philip Grey

K

Natasha Mostert
Speedball

The most terrifying word in the writer's lexicon begins with B. The concept it symbolizes fills me with such superstitious dread, I have difficulty speaking its name. There it sits: brooding, bulky, perched perilously somewhere inside my temporal lobe. It is heavy with expectations, doubts, intentions, self-criticism... so heavy, in fact, that it constantly threatens to topple over and crash onto the page.

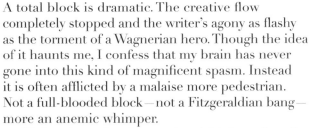

A total block is dramatic. The creative flow completely stopped and the writer's agony as flashy as the torment of a Wagnerian hero. Though the idea of it haunts me, I confess that my brain has never gone into this kind of magnificent spasm. Instead it is often afflicted by a malaise more pedestrian. Not a full-blooded block—not a Fitzgeraldian bang— more an anemic whimper.

Fitting then, that the words, which best describe my affliction of the mind all start with a sibilant: sag, slump, sluggish, scared…

A scared brain. How to turn a mouse into a warrior?

Against the wall of my study hangs a boxer's speedball. Its swollen plumlike shape is sexy and potent. It beckons me several times a day. At first, when I touch the ball the beat it produces is hesitant. It is not easy—this rhythmic tapping out of a triplet beat, this rolling firing pattern of the muscles of the upper arms and chest. After the first few seconds the stuttering ball will begin to hum, by the end of a two-minute round it sings. And your brain responds to the music. No more sagging and slumping, but swaying and spinning…

There is something pleasing about the conceit of a boxing speedball turned into a writing tool. Novel writing is not a team sport. Neither is boxing. The boxer steps into the ring alone and stands or falls by his own skills and strength. Like the writer. And like the fighter, the novelist obsessively searches for the sweet punch.

Is not the brain shaped like a pair of boxing gloves?

Hanif Kureishi
The Pens

The place I write is a room on the first floor of my house in West London, where I have two old computers and am surrounded by books, CDs, photographs, and children's drawings, as well as a drawing of Dad by my mother. I prefer to write by hand rather than type; the movement of the arm seems closer to drawing—doodling, rather— and to inner movement. Ultimately these are habits; daily repetitions. A new thing is an excuse for another thing the same. Then you know where you are. Beckett is full of these obsessions—you might call his an aesthetic of futile repetitions.

Don't think I haven't noticed that many artists are as compelled by the rituals which surround their art—silence, covering paper, screwing it up, tossing it in the bin—as much as by the matter itself. After a few years it becomes obvious that the art is there to serve the ritual, which is everything. If you aren't an obsessive, you can't be an artist, however imaginative you might be.

Harpster Brush
Claude Oolong

Stein Verkers

Jack Bartin

Bobert Mitterwald

Claus Brush

Mipster Backport

Garimore Clothatch

Calvin Lindy

Dr. Fandling

Lazlo Jury

Walter Jury

Barry Favors

Joey California

Ed Haze

Fritz John

Harpster Dewitt

Hewitt Favors

Billy Detmer

Sparkla

Rod Pinfruit

Itsy Dall

Steven Morgenlander

Falvin Teafinder

Fewis Rettering

Salvin Copperminer

Cole Bayzwaite

Carlton Bark

Earl Louis Reeg

Jester Bundy

Sivling Lorch

Betty Littolat

Wheatniz Betterly

Malvin Toydance

Jonathan Lethem
Names

Sterson Mawkus

Morgan Mefner

Magly

Storton Zeglander

Davis Clome

Grover Testafer

Brown Green

Orton Angwine

Empress Forshort

Sterson Mawkus

Pansy Greenleaf

Singlebane

Evan Indome

Ergen Hutcare

Smoky Vales

Frankie Argyle

Metcalf Ditmar

Zimmy Milkwater

Holt Carbondale

Sterling Daleholt

Ding Hotland

Lyle Catson

Kyle Brush

Gilligan Lafcart

Cumbler

Inhaul

Wally Bendale

Phoneblum

Eugene Tree

Walter Tree

Rayhew

George Bendale

For the first seven or eight years of my serious attempts to write—beginning almost twenty-five years ago—I typed out sheets of potential character names and threw them into a file, labeled "names." In the file are dozens of these sheets, and hundreds of names (or versions, recursions, or fragments of names). For each name that has ever found a home in a novel or story there are dozens that never have, and likely never will.

At some point, perhaps a decade ago, my production of the names began to diminish, as if in acknowledgment of this disproportion, or in despair at the hopelessness of these "unborn" characters. Anyway, more and more I found that when I began a story or novel I would no longer look in the "names" file, but rather invent new names on the spot. So the file has become a relic and a talisman, a souvenir of the jubilant and hyperproductive nature of my early writing life.

The sheet beginning with the name "Harpster Brush" is one of the very oldest, and most cherished. On it appears, fully formed, as if by some miracle, the names "Grover Testafer," "Pansy Greenleaf," and "Orton Angwine," as well as the name elements "Phoneblum," "Walter," "Barry," "Joey," "Morgenlander," and "Metcalf": pretty much the whole cast of my first novel, *Gun, with Occasional Music*. To see them there in such nascent form is, for me, like recognizing a bunch of later-to-be-famous actors in their high school yearbook photos. Because so many from this page sprang to life, the others seem charged as well: shouldn't there be a place for "Claude Oolong" or "Malvin Toydance" somewhere, eventually? Yet perhaps if I ever gave a home to every name on this sheet I'd be done, and have to find a new line of work.

David Guterson
Driving

I used to have a lot of clear ideas about writing, but as time has gone on I've had to acknowledge the difference between my ideas about it and reality. What actually occurs when I write has no form or principle. I don't know what's going to happen or how it will happen, and most of the time I'm either happily or unhappily surprised by what's going on as opposed to being in charge of it.

I was staying with a friend in Deer Park once, north of Spokane, and got up at three and took a shower and crept out of the house and drove away. It was a Sunday morning and so early that all the traffic lights on Division Street were blinking. I was just awake and hadn't spoken a word and so the driving was like dreaming. In the dream I was crossing my home state. Between Sprague and Ritzville there was plenty of darkness except that a little of the glow from my dashboard lights illuminated the carved bear figurines tucked into the curve of my windshield. On this day off my writing I began to think about my novel-in-progress and by the time I got to Ritzville I had to pull off the interstate, not only to buy a notebook but to cry because I felt badly for some of the people in my book. Inside the mini-mart, two young duck or goose hunters dressed in camouflage gear were getting self-serve coffee, and while I picked out a notebook their conversation—which was frankly, I thought, a lot of idle foolishness—distracted me, and then I had to stand behind them in a line to make my purchase and, it couldn't be helped, listen to more of their sadistic banter underneath all of that mini-mart wattage. You would think this interlude would break the spell, but the road toward Othello was so overwhelmingly perfect in the darkness that the world dissipated within 15 minutes and I was "writing" again.

Marie Darrieussecq
Alphabets

The small square alphabet was embroidered by my Basque great-grandmother, Amaxie Jeanne, in 1899. She was eight years old at the time. The large square alphabet was made in 1921 by her daughter, my Basque grandmother, Amaxie Adine, when she was seven. The small rectangular one is the work of their granddaughter and daughter respectively—my mother, Amaxie Janine, my children's grandmother. My great-grandmother and grandmother were forbidden from speaking Basque at school, and my mother spoke only Basque up until she first went to school at the age of nine. We Basques are the savages of Europe. Ethnologists come and visit us.

Photo by Kristine Thiemann

These Basque women alphabet-makers were violently taught to speak French at school through the feminine rite of passage that is embroidery. And now I write under their patronage, in that fabulous foreign language of French.

The fourth alphabet—the one with "oui," "non," and "au revoir" on it—is a ouija board, for talking to spirits. I had been looking for a ouija board at a conference in Iceland (a deadly serious one, somewhere between psychoanalysis, aesthetics, and folk tradition) where I had been planning to give a paper on the terribly romantic tradition of communicating with the spirit world. That was the first time I ever set foot in a shop selling esoterica, only to be told that ouija boards will set you back several hundred euros. And so I asked my father to draw me one. The idea is to place a glass on top of the board with your finger on top. You let the glass slide from letter to letter whilst invoking a spirit, and it makes words. Give it a try!

The photocopy of a photo in black and white shows my publisher Paul Otchakovsky and me in 1996, shooting cuddly-toy pigs at a fair in Bordeaux.

The little scene in painted wood is something I bought in Mexico during the Day of the Dead festival that takes place there around Halloween time. It shows two little skeletons playing pool with skulls for balls. Underneath the table is a dog, faithfully waiting for the game to finish.

The radiator that the little scene is resting on is just your common or garden cast iron one painted white. The radiator is something I shan't mind parting with next time I move house.

Translated by Suzanne Dow

Nicole Krauss
A Body Plummeting Through the Air

When I was nineteen I went to the National Portrait Gallery in London and saw a lithograph of Samuel Beckett. The artist, Tom Phillips, had drawn him from behind as he sat in the front row watching a rehearsal of *Waiting for Godot*, proving that the back of Beckett's head, guarded by two majestic ears, was just as distinctive as his face. At the bottom Phillips had printed a line from another of Beckett's plays: NO MATTER. TRY AGAIN. FAIL AGAIN. FAIL BETTER. Beckett was, and still is, one of my literary heroes. By that point I'd read all the plays, and was steadily burrowing my way through the novels.

NO MATTER · TRY AGAIN
FAIL AGAIN · FAIL BETTER

Downstairs in the museum shop, I found that they had a postcard of the lithograph. For the next four years it followed me through a long succession of student rooms, accumulating a steady build-up of blue-tack on the reverse.

I loved it, but for a long time I didn't get it. I thought I got it—the depressive's wry humor, resigned to making a bollocks of it given the inadequacy of language, "I can't go on, I must go on, I will go on," etc.—but really I didn't. The truth was that I wanted more than anything to succeed at becoming a writer. And because there seemed to me to be a standard for that—being published—I only embraced the line about failure in that self-conscious, romantic way that one embraces quotations by great writers: as profound but, ultimately, rhetorical. As for me, I still hoped to succeed.

And I suppose that according to those early minimalist standards, I did. That year my first poems were published, and some years later my first novel. But it didn't take me long to realize that publishing had very little to do with succeeding as a writer, at least in the ways that mattered. Mostly it just made me starkly aware of how inadequate everything I'd ever written was. Not because anyone said so, but because I knew it to be so, and seeing the words in print between two cloth-bound covers didn't do anything to magically transform them. In the months between publishing my first novel and beginning my second, I found myself seriously questioning whether I should be a writer at all.

Somewhere along the way I lost the postcard. But a few weeks after that first novel was published, I found a black and white photograph at the Chelsea flea market, taken sometime in the late forties. Shot from a small plane, it's a view of two parachuters making their descent toward a patchwork landscape of snow and dirt fields. The parachute of the first jumper has already ballooned open, the strings are taut, his body limp as he falls evenly through space. It won't be long now until he touches the ground. The other has just leapt from the plane seconds ago, his legs thrust out in front of him, the strings of his parachute unfurling. For now he's still falling by his own weight; the parachute has yet to catch him in its invisible lasso, to yank him back from the most stupendous disaster. It's one of the most exhilarating images I've ever seen: a body plummeting through the air above a field of snow. How free, and afraid, and alive he must feel. Whenever I look at it, where it hangs above my desk, it makes me want to write.

Photo by Garrett Linn

FRANK SINATRA

in the wee small hours

Neil LaBute
In the Wee Small Hours

I'm a big believer in writing only when the mood hits me, when inspiration comes right up and kicks my ass back into a chair and says, "Get to it!" I hate staring at an empty field of white— I'm only myself when it starts to fill up with glorious words (even semi-glorious words will do). One thing that I can always count on to inspire me, however, is the fifty-odd minutes of musical woe that Frank Sinatra spins on his album, *In the Wee Small Hours*. It's not just the music—which absolutely takes my breath away—but even the cover art can do the trick: Frank, with a trademark fedora tilted back on his head and holding a burning cigarette, looking down and forlorn as a Hopper-esque landscape spreads itself out behind him. Take another glance at his expression—I know it's only a drawing, but I'll be damned if the real Frank wasn't captured there with those pens and ink. It's around that time that "Glad to be Unhappy" begins to play. And then the magic begins to happen for me. Hey, if St. Francis can feel a little bummed at times, then all is right with the world.

Iain Sinclair
The Monkey's Jaw

My father kept his better books in glass-fronted cases that must have been a newspaper offer, in the years after the war; when austerity edged toward conspicuous consumption. They fascinated me, those spines. The colors, the shapes. The sliding doors were stiff. The whole deal was as much a unit of display as a working library. Yellowback Austin Freeman crime novels. Edgar Wallace. Jack the Ripper. The blue-gray run of that frequently consulted oracle, Chambers's Encyclopaedia (in XV volumes with six supplements).

Sawdust Caesar with its fearsome portrait of Mussolini. The slim book on Cuba we both bought, at the same sale, and never read. A fat green *Ulysses*. Wyndham Lewis's *The Apes of God* (the revised edition, in monkey dust jacket). Most of Conan Doyle in compendium form. A single leather-bound volume, my great-grandfather's Peruvian expedition (with fold-out map).

On top of the bookcase sat a collection of curious objects: grave goods from South America, a mummified head (fake), a cigar cabinet (my father never smoked cigars), a silver monkey sitting on a pile of books. All these things, along with the random library, demanded a linking narrative. If there had been time, perhaps, my father would have provided it. He worked long hours, weekends and night calls, as a GP in a Welsh mining town. He limited himself to anecdotes, sinister comedies that had the crafted shape of tales by W.W. Jacobs or Saki.

After his death, the clear-out, the monkey came with me to London. To the Hackney room where it still remains — and where I wrote my first books. It's heavy, cold, this creature. Made from cast iron and then dipped in a layer of silver that is chipping away. It's a Rodin parody, a blind animal contemplating a human skull. It sits, cross-legged, on three books (of diminishing thickness). The Bible, undoubtedly — and then, I would guess, Darwin's *On the Origin of Species by Means of Natural Selection*. And one other, uncredited, still to be written. Monkey as Hamlet: a *Punch* cartoon ridiculing evolution. The hair, center-parted, makes this ape of god look pathetically *fin de siècle*: Aubrey Beardsley in a Tom Jones chest-wig.

It took me years to understand the metaphor: it was a literal "monkey on my back." I was doomed to add to the book mountain until the modest stack grew into a model of the Empire State Building. With the monkey as King Kong (a primitive hulk at the base of my consciousness).

Poor Jacko watches that skull like the clock of fate, an hourglass of sand in a Viking drinking vessel. And, in the curve of the polished silver memento mori, I saw my own reflection, hammering away at a defunct typewriter. A Faustian contract: heredity. An inherited nonconformist work ethic. Write or die. Write *and* die. Grow into the thing the monkey contemplates with its pinprick eyes.

The jaw is broken, a hinge. You can lift the monkey's cranium, as for a decadent feast, and reveal a metal stub. A cylinder like a bullet — for a solitary game: Russian roulette. It's a cigarette lighter, but it doesn't light. Not for me. It sits alongside a cigar cabinet in which there are no cigars. The dust of leaves and the dust of vanished books.

In the W.W. Jacobs story, "The Monkey's Paw," a man wishes his son back to life. Part of the psychic outwash that followed the First War. Now there is a scratching sound in my shadowy room. Squirrels in the eaves? What if, after all these years, the flint should strike? What shapes would I see by the yellow flame in the monkey's head? The winter dead come to the door to listen. They can hear the clatter of that ventriloquised jaw as I retell the story the old ones have left me.

Photo by Philip Grey

Tash Aw
The Rituals of Tea

Trawling aimlessly through the library some years ago, I discovered Luk Yu's eighth-century *Tea Classics*, the definitive guide to Chinese tea. Here are some of his (quite firm) suggestions for making the perfect cup of tea:

* Use only water from mountain streams (though never from water that falls in cascades or gushes from springs).
* When the water boils it should look like fish eyes and give off but a hint of noise.
* During the second stage of boiling, draw off a ladle of water and stir the water with bamboo pincers; do not allow the water to overboil.

In London, my attempt to adapt and modernize these rules has become an obsession. I can just about discern the point at which the water in my kettle chatters like a bubbling spring (because my ear is pressed dangerously close to it), but how can I tell when it looks like innumerable pearls strung together? Easy: by buying a see-through plastic kettle off eBay. Tea doesn't froth delicately when poured into the bowl? Adjust hard water filter. The surface of my tea rarely reminds me of clouds drifting across a clear blue sky, I admit, but the other day it *did* resemble overlapping fish scales, which is almost as good.

I start my working day with a cup of tea. The level of attention I give to the making of each morning's pot depends on how well my work is progressing, how optimistic I feel about that day's writing. Usually there isn't a great deal of fuss; thirst outweighs ceremony and I'm still half asleep. Everyone has a start-of-the-day ritual, and mine is watching tea leaves unfurl. Later in the morning and throughout the day I make more tea. A couple of good paragraphs may be celebrated by expensive tea drunk from decent cups, while a slump in creativity might lead to an elaborate multi-stage tea-brewing process that takes half an hour: sip, decide it's not good enough, throw away, start again. And again. On the days when the tea is flat and slightly bitter I know the writing process will be similar. But sometimes, on a particularly good day, I am able to look into my tea bowl and see floating duckweed at the beginning of time. Honestly.

Photo by Philip Grey

William Fiennes
A Cypress Cone

I don't have a desk of my own. I'm working in a friend's house in Stockwell, where I have the use of a polished gate-leg table in the basement room, a few of my books scattered beneath the jurisdiction of an Anglepoise. The patch of lawn I can see through the square sash window nags at my attention, because there's a fox den in the garden and I've heard that sometimes you can see fox cubs playing on the grass, and this rumor alone is enough to make the lawn come alive with possibility, like a stage immediately before the first actors walk out onto it. Apart from my books and papers, the only thing I've brought with me to clutter the table beneath the lordly Anglepoise is a cypress cone—walnut-sized, with roughly hexagonal plates growing off a central stem—that my mother picked up for me off one of the paths in Chekhov's garden in Yalta, which she and my father had visited as part of the Tsars and Sultans cruise of the Black Sea to which they'd treated themselves on his eightieth birthday. They'd embarked in Istanbul and sailed round anti-clockwise to Thessaloniki via Trabzon, Odessa, Constanta, and Nessebur, and they talked afterward about the derelict submarines at Sevastopol, the battlefield at Balaklava, the Crimea's unexpected tea plantations and desolate sanatoria, the copper-sulphate color of the Black Sea itself, and the view you got from the hill of Hissarlik over the plains and megarons of Troy, but none of this was as interesting to me as the story of their visit to Chekhov's house in Yalta, the "White Dacha" to which he'd moved in 1898 in the hope of recovery or at least relief from tuberculosis, and where he'd finished *The Cherry Orchard* and written such stories as "The Lady with the Dog" and "In the Ravine" and "The Bishop"—his home until he died, six years later, in the German resort of Badenweiler, at the age of forty-four.

Sometimes I think about the desk I'm going to have one day, and although the design of this utopian workstation changes each time I revisit it, the cypress cone is always there—my desk's first distinguishing mark; the tiny, dense nucleus of the entire room. I imagine the simplicity of oak planks laid across trestles, a kitchen table scored with knife marks, the vast Victorian pedestal desk that sat like Marble Arch in the middle of my grandfather's study and seemed to take several minutes to walk around—these dream desks variously furnished with treasured books, photographs, letters, cards, and a low-wattage lamp of limited range, so that while the rest of the room remains in shadow, the desk itself inhabits a gentle, specific light, as local as a mood—a little world of thought and feeling which you can step into, the heights of table and chair so precisely adjusted that you and the desk seem to nest into one another, a perfect fit. The cypress cone is lovely to handle and contemplate—as the cone dried and aged, the hexagonal plates drew apart, allowing the seeds to escape, and you can see white flecks inside where seeds were originally berthed—but its presence is more than botanical. In his Yalta garden Chekhov planted cherries, almonds, apricots, mulberries, palms, figs, birches, bamboos, and cedars; it's likely he planted the cypress that produced the cone my mother picked up off the path, the woody jewel in which all my dreams of a writer's desk are concentrated. Sometimes I think that having the right desk would unlock everything, that sitting down at the right desk would grant immediate access to images and language far beyond the reach of ordinary tables. I haven't found it. All I have is the cypress cone.

T°ny D'S°uza
The Lights of My Writing Life

I get very nervous in the hour or two before it's time to write. I get butterflies in my stomach, and often feel nauseous, especially if I'm near completion of a draft. At that point, I'll have put a lot of emotion and energy into the piece and I can feel the payoff close at hand. I get nervous because I need the Muse to show up, and I have no control over that. I drink a beer or two or four, and smoke cigarettes, to calm myself down and get to the writing. It's neither healthy nor wise, but it works for me.

O

Writing well is so important to me that I put it before health, relationships, everything. It's not a recipe I want to pawn off as hip, cool, funny— I'm not trying to make a statement—and I don't recommend it. It's simply my process.

My beer of choice in the U.S. is Miller Lite. It doesn't make me too drunk not to work, and it doesn't give me unreasonable hangovers. It's also very affordable. Abroad, I'll drink whatever cheap pilsner is most like Miller Lite. I smoke Camel Light cigarettes because I like their burning pace and flavor.

As I write, I'll step outside every 40 minutes or so and have a smoke and sip and contemplate the stars from my porch or yard or balcony or beach, wherever I happen to be. The length of a cigarette gives me enough time to work through whatever stump or knot I've come across in the writing. Then I go back in to it.

The alcohol loosens me up, dampens the butterflies, and releases my ego's grip on my subconscious. Maybe I could reach those places I need to be without it, but I don't know that.

I don't smoke at all when I'm not writing, and I don't like to drink ceaselessly. But the idea of writing without a six-pack of Miller Lite bottles and a half dozen Camel Light cigarettes seems too tortuous to me to even try. If we ever meet, however, for god's sake buy me a pint of Stella Artois.

Claire Messud

.005

For reasons that I can only partially explain, I always write fiction by hand, on graph paper — this graph paper — with a very particular pen. The paper is from a large pad with a yellow card cover, manufactured by Rhodia; and when I first started writing, now twenty years ago, these pads were only readily available in Europe. Now — presumably because I am not alone in the pleasure and reassurance I take in their orderly squares, and in the particularly smooth texture of the paper itself — they can be found at most good stationers in big cities in the United States, which is a relief to my naturally anxious self, and which means I don't have to return from ~~nearly~~ every European trip with a suitcase weighted down by paper. [As for the pens: I've used a number of them over the years, all mercifully inexpensive and easy to replace, their chief qualification being the fineness of their point. Since moving to Cambridge, Massachusetts several years ago, I've settled upon a particular little pen, found in the art section of a local shop. It's called a Pigma Micron (even its name is pleasing to me) + I choose the finest nib they offer, .005. I have to be careful with them, though, because my children like to draw with them, and inevitably flatten the tiny felt tip, or break it off, rendering the pen useless. [By now, I know how many words I get to a line, how many typed pages to a handwritten page, and surely part of my attachment to this writing habit lies therein. I do not break for paragraphs, but instead indicate them with a little bracket: [. I make insertions using other little symbols (＊ or ✶) to direct me to the additional passage when I come back to type; and I write on the backs of pages only when adding things in. Of course, I don't really have margins, so can't say I make use of them; but can, if need be, write in lines above or below the main text. Crossing out is no problem; ~~not~~ and I like, with hand-writing, that I always have in front of me the traces of what I have discarded. An entire novel usually takes up a single notebook, not quite fully: there are 80 pages in each pad. I like to think that I don't waste paper, or not too much of it.

Jake Arnott
*My Grandmother
the Dancer*

This picture has followed me around for the last decade and a half. I've hung it in the kitchen of wherever I lived at that time. Maybe because I remember her cooking, fixing an early-evening gin and tonic, telling stories. It's a photograph of my grandmother in Paris, sometime in the late twenties, when she worked in a nightclub as a showgirl. I remember finding it with her as she was sorting out a chaotic bundle of memories. She pointed out that the costume was for a burlesque number that had a hunt theme. Note the stylized riding cap and gloves, the kinky fur-trimmed boots, the diamante riding crop. It could have been taken when she was at the Moulin Rouge or the Folies Bergères—she worked at both between 1927 and 1928. She left bits of a diary, hastily scribbled, absurdly terse. Here's some of February 1927, when she was at the Moulin Rouge:

Tuesday, 1 February
complet, sandwich

Wednesday, 2 February
bain

Thursday, 3 February
no bath, complet

Friday, 4 February
no bath

Saturday, 5 February
complet, bain

Sunday, 6 February
1 café complet, 4 chocolates, 6 biscuits

Monday, 7 February
bath, 2 pommes, 2 biscuits

Tuesday, 8 February
3 chocolates, 1 apple, 2 biscuits

Sunday, 13 February
danced but sat precariously on 1 ladder

Monday, 14 February
complet, bain, fell through ladder

Tuesday, 15 February
complet, fell through ladder,
made resolve not to eat
chocolates, bought jumper.

One hopes that she was eating a little more than she recorded, but you know what dancers are like. There are regular entries that indicate the dangers of her workplace ("2 stagehands hurt, sent to hospital," "stagehand fell from flies onto a fireman," "chorus boy fell downstairs, badly hurt"—all in one month), but frustratingly scant details of her life then. I remember the stories she told me decades later in her house in Clapham. I recall a tough and rather frightening woman who had spent all her working life in show business and was still running after Routemaster buses in her seventies. I love this picture because it catches her at her most glamorous. When the writer's life seems at its dullest I can remind myself that I'm in show business too. That she lived so much and wrote down so little has perhaps been a provocation to me. One day I'll tell her stories. When I'm good enough to do her justice.

Matt Thorne
Walking

Six or seven years ago I was giving a reading in Manchester with a couple of other authors. We were all new enough to the game to still be excited by the prospect of a night in a hotel and a decent audience. After the show we invited the booksellers and a few of the audience back to our hotel room for a party. Around 4 a.m. a woman turned to me and said, "You have writer's shoes."

I didn't know what she meant and asked her to explain, assuming it was an insult. "They're worn down," she said, "they look like you spend a long time walking around in the rain." She was right. I couldn't work out whether it was an insult or a compliment, but it was definitely true. Ever since I was a kid I've spent a lot of time walking and it's an important part of my writing process. I'm not one of those hearty types who go up mountains, or an occultist psychogeographer: my walks are strictly urban, and mostly mundane. I walk the same route into town every time and if I feel up to it come back the same way.

After the London tube bombings, I started bumping into other writers I know along this route, outside the British Library or heading down Tottenham Court Road. People were too frightened to take buses or tubes for a while, and although this was a terrible thing, bumping into people always lifts my mood, and makes the city feel like a close community. I don't mind walking with other people, but I get my best thinking done alone. The nicest times are coming back from a party or a club at midnight with a head full of ideas, working them out on the way home and sitting down at the desk to write through the early hours.

Michel Faber
Krautrock

An HB pencil sharpened exactly halfway between sharpness and bluntness. A beloved old office chair with armrests at a 25° angle. A cup of filter coffee, served at exactly 8:15 in the morning, along with a blueberry danish from my favorite baker. Notepaper in the long-superseded foolscap size, ruled faint, each page marked at the top right-hand corner with the date in red pen. A leather necklace I was once given by a shaman in Dakota, without which I feel I cannot connect with the mysterious forces of literary creativity.

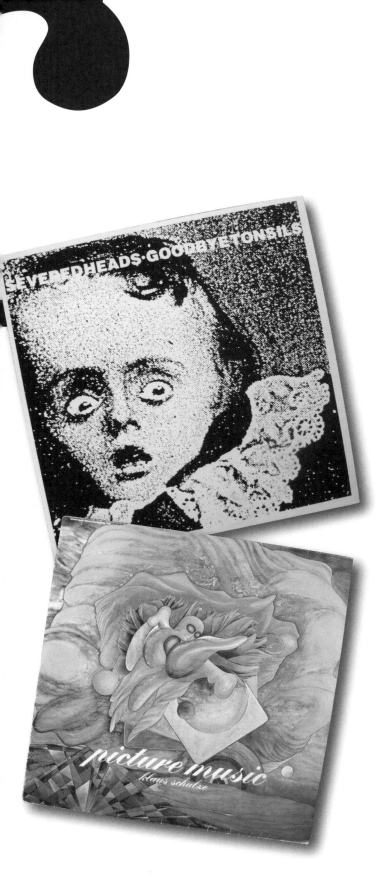

Jesus Christ, why not throw in a turtle aquarium, a belly dancer, and a rainbow outside the bloody window too? What does a writer *really* need in order to work?

Me, I need nothing special. I use a computer. Don't ask me what brand it is, I couldn't care less. What time in the morning do I start work? Whenever I wake up. What do I eat? Whatever's around. What are my bare minimum requirements? Solitude, and enough light to see the screen. Any talismans, lucky ornaments, superstitious procedures? Nope.

Mind you, I want to enjoy myself while I'm writing, and my most constant source of enjoyment is music. So, I've set up my workspace to give me easy access to the jazz-rock, prog rock, avant-garde electronica, and Krautrock that I adore. A turntable sits next to the keyboard. A stack of music equipment looms inches from my left shoulder. Cassettes are piled near my ankles. The drawers of my desk are stuffed with CDs. LP sleeves litter the desk. What influence does this music have on my writing? Some, I suppose. The eerie yet poignant atmosphere of a story like "The Fahrenheit Twins" is the literary equivalent of the vibe I feel coming off sublime Krautrock albums by Neu, Cluster, or Klaus Schulze.

Mainly, though, I use music to sharpen up my own focus. When I was writing my Victorian opus *The Crimson Petal and the White*, I didn't play 19th-century music to "get me in the mood." I played Miles Davis (his electric funk period), Mahavishnu Orchestra, Trans-Global Underground, Severed Heads, Nurse With Wound. I did this not merely because I love this stuff. I did it because I'm wary of filling the air around me with the same ingredients as I'm trying to put into my prose. I don't want to fool myself into thinking I've captured something on the page when, in reality, it's swirling around the room. My most violent, angst-infused prose was written to a soundtrack of happy, serene music. And vice versa.

Now excuse me while I turn the record over.

Joyce Carol Oates
Portrait

In my study, I am surrounded by numerous artworks, some of them original and most of them reproductions (of paintings by, for instance, Matisse, Monet, Munch, the Canadian Tom Thomson). There are a number of photographs of family members and friends, which provide some measure of consolation, comfort, or emotional support of the kind we all need, writers or not. The most prized of the original works of art is an impressionistic portrait of me by the artist Gloria Vanderbilt, who is a close friend living in New York City. The portrait seems to me enigmatic and haunting, an image that asks a question, which I hope might be true for my own writing. It's also a testament to a very special friendship. I'm not at all a visual artist but am inspired by the genius of others for rendering subtle and mysterious states in visual terms.

Jay McInerney
An Axe in My Hand

This is an Acheulian hand axe, approximately a half million years old, crafted by Homo Erectus, which was given to me by my friend Anthony Hamilton Russell, who found it on his farm in Walker Bay, South Africa. The design of this hand axe was pretty consistent for more than a million years. I like to heft it and hold it between paragraphs. It fits the palm beautifully. It reminds me of a friend and a beautiful landscape; sometimes I try to imagine its maker and his world.

Tibor Fischer

If you are willing to accept a one-word contribution, you can have it: money.

Nick Laird

Cocktails from Water and Ice

I have no set routine for writing. I write every day if
I can, and if I'm working on a novel I try and get a
certain number of words on the page before it gets dark.
And then, in the evening, if something has stuck in my
head, what Berryman, in "Dream Song 29," calls "the
little cough somewhere, an odor, a chime," I tend to
write poems. If it goes well I'll still be sitting there at
three in the morning, rearranging words on the screen.

The walls of my study are covered in pictures and photographs and maps and poems. A small plastic spirit level is balanced on top of my computer screen and I like the bubble to be dead center in it. Quotes from Churchill ("Continuous effort, not strength or intelligence...") and, I think, Flaubert ("The words are like hair: they shine with combing") are Blu-Tacked to the bottom of the monitor. I tend to work in silence, or what passes for silence in London (birdsong, engines revving, next door's stereo, the trains rumbling past) and sometimes I wear foam earplugs. Occasionally I'll play classical music on iTunes. I got bored with checking my email and surfing the web so a year ago I cut through my internet cable with a pair of nail scissors.

Although the room is full of souvenirs, or what my family calls tat, there's one thing I like to have to hand. It's a small bracelet I made several years ago in Wellington, New Zealand. I was out visiting my sister, who likes to make jewelry, and we'd been to a bead shop. I bought a bag of letter beads and set about making some elastic bracelets with gnomic messages. This one paraphrases a line from a favorite poem, Frank O'Hara's "Animals," and says "cocktails from water and ice." The actual line is "we could manage cocktails out of ice and water" and either I misremembered it or didn't have the right letters. It's not a bad metaphor for writing, I think, and if I'm sitting staring into space I sometimes find myself clicking the little plastic letters through like rosary beads.

ZZ Packer
Nat Love

This is a picture of Nat Love, probably the most famous black cowboy who roped and wrangled cattle in the West after the Civil War. I've always been fascinated by this picture of him, the pose with all his gear, as if determined to live up to all his tall tales; the picture eventually led to me writing a novel about the Buffalo Soldiers (black men who served as infantry and cavalry) during the same "Old West" period. The picture has variously been a postcard on my desk to a large photograph hanging above my desk. Not pictured: coffee.

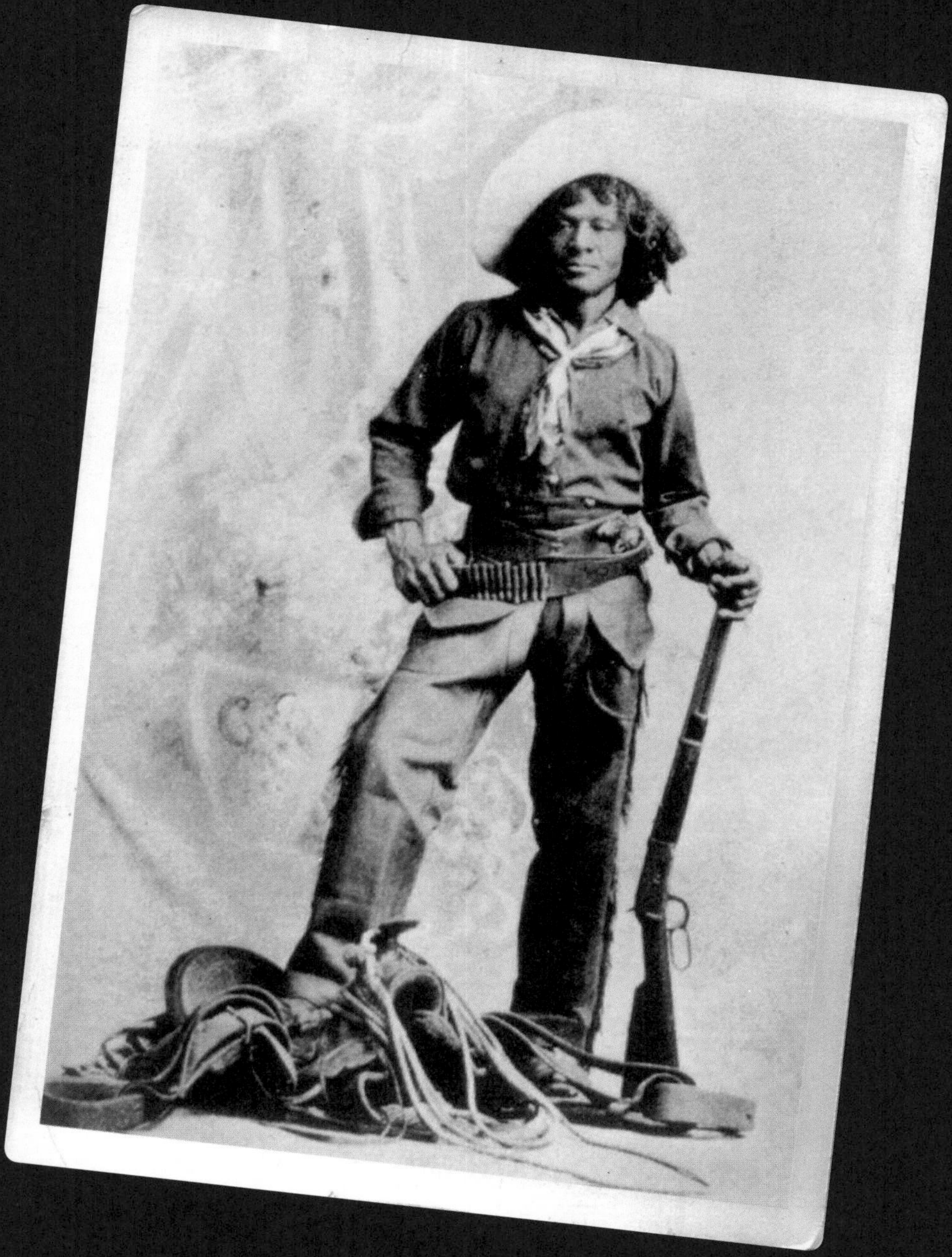

Javier Marías
"This Childish Task"

Almost all my shelves are safeguarded, protected, defended by little lead soldiers from different armies and disparate eras—and in one case by a population of civilians, made not of lead but a tough, high-quality German plastic. Just as the soldiers are arranged in file, and either all of the same size or logically proportioned in relation to one another (which is true whether they're on foot, horseback, or riding camels), the civilians intermingle chaotically and come from different walks of existence (there are even wild animals and dancing couples). Some seem enormous next to others, this group Lilliputian compared to that one. I suspect that all this is not entirely fortuitous, although I tend to think of it that way. In civilian society everything is less highly ordered; it is more muddled, there's no requirement for discipline to exist (and if it does it means we're under a dictatorial regime, such as I suffered in Spain during the first twenty-four years of my life: never again, please), and all the frivolities, inconsistencies, and monstrosities are acceptable, so to speak. In armies that's not an option, or at least it's inadvisable, just as in novels.

I guess there are two sides to my affinity for miniature worlds: there's the childish innocence of it, and the literary dimension—though perhaps these are ultimately the same thing. It certainly stems in part from my childhood. Children have an enormous capacity to become obsessed with, and what's more, actually step inside and immerse themselves in very small things, breathing a fictional life into them. In days gone by, war and combat would be the backdrop of choice for young boys' fantasies, which were acted out with toy soldiers and (if a boy was lucky) a fort which the Indians would besiege relentlessly; while young girls, I imagine, focused on or became transfixed by the tininess of doll houses (or this was the general rule, though of course there were always exceptions and deviations: war-loving girls and more domesticated boys). At any rate, this is how countless children took their first steps into fiction. By which I mean creative fiction, fiction invented by them, fiction where anything is possible, fiction which forces them to conjure up stories, adventures, fables, however schematic and imitative these might be; while

comics, films, and books represent a fiction which is received or inherited, becoming in due course a model and a stimulus for creation and re-creation. And thinking about it, those games where one decided the fate of one's soldiers or dolls, following specific rules and always striving for verisimilitude in every imagined scene, were probably the first serious step toward writing fiction.

So if my shelves are crowded with lead soldiers I think it's partly because I refuse to lose sight entirely of the humble origins of the books I write. Keeping them present, right in front of my eyes, in adult life, is to some extent a way of remembering, over the weeks and years, the childishness of my vocation; a healthy way of keeping it in check (for there's nothing more perilous for a writer than taking himself too seriously, believing that he is carrying out an important—let alone transcendental—task), and it's also an act of loyalty. I will never forget those lines by Robert Louis Stevenson where, comparing himself to his lighthouse-building ancestors, he cannot but feel the insignificance of his calling, the insignificance of being a writer, and beseeches a little sympathy: "Say not of me that weakly I declined / The labors of my sires, and fled the sea, / The towers we founded and the lamps we lit, / To play at home with paper like a child."

I try not to get too caught up in the knowledge that this is really all I do—dedicate myself "to this childish task," to use Stevenson's words from the same poem. But I like to keep the probable root of my calling in front of me, to have it material and corporeal in that army of little figures who, though silent, expectant, and motionless, always seem—just like the characters in a novel when they're first created—as if they might any second start walking about, break into conversation, or, indeed, become the subjects of some story which only I could relate.

Translated by Andrew Staffell

Ahdaf Soueif

Akhenaten

Can a poet and philosopher also be an effective ruler? Is it impossible to be both a good person and a good politician? What is "good" anyway and who is it good for? These questions crowd your head when you contemplate Akhenaten (1352–1336 BC), a king who was rooted in tradition but also believed in innovation, in "progress." For him, one was born of the other. The act he is most famous (or infamous) for—the promotion of the worship of the Aten—was the imaginative sequel of a dream dreamed by his grandfather, Tuthmosis IV. His placing of his wife, Nefertiti, as co-monarch side by side with him on the throne was consistent with Egyptian Law which saw men and women as equal. His (in)formal royal portraiture of himself with his infant daughters playing on his knee expressed the culture's well-publicized celebration of children. His reign let loose an eruption of brilliant and original art. Yet he is deemed to have failed.

He was a man of questing and intelligent spirituality, a man who both loved and liked women and was decent on gender issues, a brilliant poet and an affectionate father and an original thinker. A man whose influence caused those around him to blossom. And yet for the state of Egypt, he was a disaster; by the time he died the treasury was empty, there were rebellions—incursions even—on the borders, and there was no clear succession. It took Akhenaten's opposite to save the day—or the millennium: Horemheb, Commander General of the army, eventually staged a coup, took the throne and shrewdly passed the succession to the family who became the Ramessides, thus not only preventing Egypt's collapse but setting the country on the path to the thousand years of the New Kingdom.

I visit Akhenaten in the Cairo Museum whenever I'm in Egypt. There's a model there of what a house in Tel el-Amarna, his capital, would have looked like. And there are the remnants of a mosaic floor. His time must have been a time of graciousness and beauty. We look at it now and we know that it was doomed, short-lived, aborted. Does that devalue it? Or does it make it more precious, bringing to mind much that is beautiful, "that opens up too easily and dies"?

Ian Hamilton, my husband, and I were walking with our two sons through Khan el-Khalili Bazaar in Cairo one summer evening seven months before we knew he had cancer and sixteen months before he died. The boys fixed on this mask of Akhenaten. I made them walk on—what a silly, touristy thing to do, to buy a fake pharaonic piece from the bazaar. But their father said "why not?" So we turned back, haggled a bit and bought it. We carried it all the way back to London where life, and death, overtook us and it sat—wrapped in a blanket—in a corner of the spare room for almost four years. When I got my act together to hang it, neither of the boys wanted it. It was childish, a piece of touristy tat; they would have none of Akhenaten's mask.

Was it the memory of that August evening? Fealty to a dead Egyptian king? Or a kind of bloody-minded housewifely thrift that made me hang it in my study? He watches over me as I write, or fail to write. Akhenaten, my ancestor. He sets trains of thought in motion. I don't know if they're distractions or inspirations. He makes me think that perhaps questions sometimes matter more than answers. And he reminds me that we—those of us who have died and those who have not yet—are part of one process; a process of feeling, questioning, and creating. We have our parts to play, and the part played by those who have died is not over while we, who connect to them, live.

Ronan Bennett
Terry's Fist

When I'm writing in my office and I turn my head
to the left and slightly behind, my gaze falls on Terry's fist.
There it sits, on a cabinet in the corner, a crudely
carved defiant fist encircled by barbed wire, at once naïve,
proud, angry, and clichéd. It was given to me by a young
prisoner I got to know some years ago as he began
a long sentence. He was despairing and troubled. His
letters were sometimes hopeful but mostly not. I learned a
little about his childhood—it was brutal and short. He
developed a serious heroin addiction inside. He carved the
wood for me in prison and added the barbed wire
when he got out. He came to my office to give it to me.

He was lost and sad, out of place among the books and papers, and, sensing his discomfort, I felt uncomfortable. I had been in prison, but that was a long time ago and my life is different now. The element of struggle is gone. Terry was out but he had new struggles ahead, harder than he or I knew.

I didn't see a lot of him. Sometimes he'd call and we'd talk but there was not a lot I could do for him. Once he called me while I was having a drink in a bar in Islington with a film producer with whom I was working. He needed some money and I said for him to come to the bar. When he arrived he needed more than I had on me so I went to the cashpoint, leaving him with my friend. I returned, gave Terry the money and he left. My friend told me after he'd gone that he'd said to her, : "I'm sorry." "What for?" she'd asked, puzzled. "For being like this," Terry said quietly. She noticed his hands, covered in jail tattoos. Embarrassed, he stuffed them in his pockets.

I didn't know it but Terry was back on heroin. To feed his habit, he borrowed for as long as he could. Then the inevitable. He pulled a couple of inept and desperate robberies in Islington and got caught. Under the three-strikes-and-you're-out rule he got life. He's still inside.

I'm writing this in a hotel room in Beverly Hills. The element of struggle for me now consists of finding a way to fix act two or trying to persuade the publisher to have another go at the book jacket. How to justify what I do? When so much is happening in the world. By claiming that fiction holds up a mirror to society? That the truths it reveals are important bulwarks of self-knowledge and understanding? That the humanistic spirit from which the arts proceed is in turn nurtured by artists' endeavors? I am constantly amazed that so little of what we produce connects with the convulsions we see around us. I am shocked by the trivia, careerism, and shallowness of what passes for the literary life.

When I look at Terry's fist I can find it hard to shake the feeling that what I am doing is a waste of time.

Arthur Bradford
The Dogs

Ever since I began writing in earnest,
I've had these two dogs around.

They are excellent companions for a writer since they don't speak and rarely interrupt me in a meaningful way. They provide just enough of a presence to ward off loneliness without hindering my ability to escape into a good solitary haze. Sometimes they will sigh and groan, especially if it is a nice day and they'd prefer to be out walking, but I don't mind that. At night, when I like to write best, they lie at my feet and sleep soundly, often twitching their legs in reaction to their silly canine dreams.

Of course, the dogs tend to creep into my work as well. My first book, *Dogwalker*, is populated with all kinds of mutts and hounds. My oldest dog, Coby, gave birth to a litter of puppies underneath my desk one winter and this couldn't help but affect what I was doing. For a while I tried to write as the puppies squirmed about underfoot, but eventually I had to move my typewriter into the kitchen and work from there.

Whenever I find myself without the dogs, it seems more difficult to write. I want to know that they are there, wishing me well, snoring at my feet. And when I've completed something worthwhile there's nothing more satisfying than rising up and telling them I'm done. They perk up immediately and jump about with glee. Then we all head outside for a good long walk. This is our reward for a job completed together.

Bruce Robinson
Tempus Omnia Revelat

Dear Dan Crowe

     Thanks for your letter and I don't know
quite what you want. I don't have any weird
habits and when I turn on the typewrite all I
hope is that I can do it. Once every ten years
I say thank you to god. As far as stuff glued
up, all I've got are three things stuck to the
front of the typewriter. I've got Sam Goldwyn's
dictum: "Pictures are for entertainment, messages
should be delivered by Western Union," and I've
got, "Write it Damn You, what Else are you good
for," which Joyce wrote, and I've got, "Tempus
Omnia Revelat," which all those side/winding
cock/suckers in New Labour better look out for.
Other than that, I don't drink to write anymore
and use aspirin. Luck with it.

          Yours faithfully

          Bruce Robinson

Nicholson Baker
Earplugs

Some years ago I bought an industrial dispenser pack of two hundred pairs of Mack's earplugs from earplugstore.com. Mostly, though, I buy them from the drug store. Recently Mack's began offering them in orange, which is less disgusting than white. I can sit anywhere, in any loud place, and work. Everything becomes twenty feet farther away than it really is. The chirping, barking, jingling cash-drawer of a world is out of reach, and therefore more precious. You must have a good seal. When you unstick your thumb from a jammed-in plug, your eardrum will make a tiny silent cry of pain, like a word in Arabic. Then you know you have a good seal.

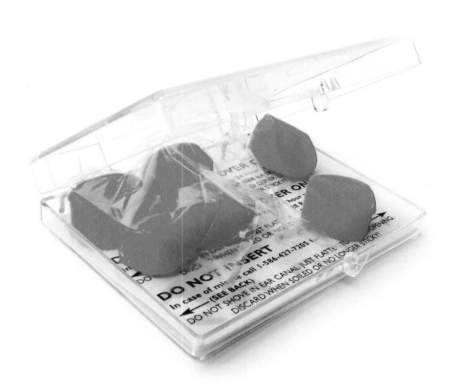

12

Tim Carvell
The Importance of My Navel

In the interests of full disclosure, I should admit up front that this essay is arriving three months past its original due date, and just barely in time for its inclusion in this book.

3

This fact is germane because it indicates that I am probably not the best person to ask about what inspires me to write. I am, however, a perfect person to ask about the best technique for removing lint from my navel—which is just one of the many techniques I use to put off the task of writing. It's a list that also includes—but is by no means limited to—watching bad reality television, Googling myself, playing online poker, skimming newspapers, eating unhealthy snacks, hanging out with my boyfriend, filling out crosswords, flipping through magazines, feeding peanuts to the squirrels in the park, napping, hitting "refresh" on my email, buying things I don't need from eBay, and staring blankly into the middle distance.

In sum, I have the attention span of a parakeet.

I envy the other writers in this book, and the magic totems they use to summon text. I wish I had something like Jonathan Franzen's squeaky chair or Nicholson Baker's earplugs. Sadly, if I had a squeaky chair, I know that I'd simply waste time trying to get it to stop squeaking, and if I bought a pair of ear plugs, I'd probably lose an afternoon trying to make them bounce off the wall into a wastebasket. For me, the only way to write is to first spend a considerable amount of time *not* writing. And that, come to think of it, may be my form of inspiration: procrastination. Sure, it may look, from a distance, like I'm lazily cleaning out my navel, but beneath the surface, my mind is getting ready to write. My navel isn't a cheap excuse for me to put off writing—rather, it's an integral partner in my writing process. That's what I tell myself, anyway.

Elif Shafak
A Purple Pen

"A bird can use its wings either to reach home or to run away from it," says my grandmother, knowing too well which of these I have opted for all these years. And she adds in haste: "Even birds take a breather to build a nest. No rest, no nest!" This is a slightly modified version of a Turkish idiom. The closest in English would probably be, "a rolling stone gathers no moss." This, I learned in due course, is very true. When you are nomadic all the time you cannot gather moss or possess inanimate objects, let alone build a home. But I prefer to believe I do have a portable home that I carry with me wherever I go: my writing.

I was born in Strasbourg, France, and spent part of my childhood in Madrid, Spain. In the years to follow I lived in Ankara, Amman, Cologne, Boston, Michigan, Arizona, among other places, and I have always been badly in love with Istanbul. Ever since I was a child, life has been a series of ruptures, arrivals, and departures. A nomad is not an immigrant. While the latter is future-oriented and aspires to settle down once and for all, the nomad lives in a perpetual present with few possessions. To live the life of a nomad means to be able to make new friendships, meet new challenges, but most of all to let go—of your possessions, of your old self. A sorrowful enrichment attends the soul along this quest. Eventually, I came to think of my writing as the major, if not the only, continuity in my life. It was this feeling that encouraged me to start writing fiction in a language other than my mother tongue. I experienced writing in English as yet another journey in itself. Of the seven books I have published so far, the last two were written in English and all were written in different places.

I am a nomad and my writing thrives upon journeys between different cultures and cities. I have never stayed in the same place long enough to start and finish a book there. I have never had the same study for long. Some of my novels I started writing in one city and ended in another, while some other novels were concluded on the road, at airports, in trains, in strange residences where I stayed for several months. Any place can be a study for me: libraries, cafes, streets, train stations… everywhere can be my writing abode. Everywhere except a neat and tidy, sterile and silent bureau. Just like every nomad, deep inside I harbor a sense of fear of orderliness and pure tranquility—both of which remind me of nothing but death.

When and if you cannot settle down and write the way I do, your relationship with inanimate objects changes altogether. There is little you can put in your suitcase and carry with you. You learn to love objects and appreciate their presence, and yet you say goodbye to them when the time comes. You learn pretty early that we human beings are not the possessors of objects. Rather, objects have a life of their own, stories of their own. Their life with us constitutes temporary stopovers on their way elsewhere. To this day some of my books are in Michigan, some in Istanbul, some in Arizona, like remnants of my life. I left beloved objects in so many places, now far away. But I somehow tend to feel they will come back when their journey is directed my way.

Being unable to accumulate bits and pieces, even the most beloved ones, in time I projected all my passion for inanimate objects onto one single article: a purple pen. Every novel that I wrote so far, I started writing with a purple pen. Although I am a devout user of computers and laptops, all my notes I take with a purple pen. I must have lost so many of them, bought so many new ones, found some old lost ones hither and thither. And yet I like to think it is always the same old purple pen that I carry in my suitcase.

"A bird can use its wings either to reach home or to run away from it," says my grandmother. I listen to her attentively. As she speaks and tells me old stories, her words leave a purple stain in my heart.

Audrey Niffenegger.
The head of a Saint

I have a small white plaster head sitting on my desk next to my computer. It's about the size of my fist. It's a woman's head, with brown glass eyes that stare calmly at nothing.

Her plaster earlobes have tiny holes meant to have earrings put through them. The head was intended to be a saint, to be colored and attached to a richly dressed figurine in a church. I don't know which saint she was supposed to be. I bought her in a shop in San Francisco; I was killing time between readings on a book tour. I remember wandering around with this little head in a shopping bag, happy to have a beautiful saint's head wrapped in shiny tissue paper. She seems to have infinite patience; her face expresses serene acceptance. I don't have much of anything left of my childhood faith, but she sits on my desk to remind me that art is made of patience. She reminds me to believe that eventually the words will come out right.

Peter Hobbs
Red and Blue Notebook

I found these particular notebooks in a beachside 7-Eleven on the Gulf coast in Florida. Just generic exercise books, I guess, and only a dollar forty-nine each (the best two dollars ninety-eight, plus tax, I ever spent), but they were perfect. Not much different to a hundred other kinds of notebook, but just different enough (maybe, I think, it's because they're not quite like the ones I always find in England. Maybe just having words like "Chattanooga," or "Dayton, Ohio" on the front is all it takes).

mead

I like them even more now that their pages are full, and they're a little battered from being carried around for a few months each. Covers almost torn free from the metal spiral. The soft blurring of paper at the corners. The bright cardboard worn and stained, and the creases inked idly in. A title for an as-yet unwritten novel scribbled, with the urgency of fear of forgetting, on the front.

It was always about the notebooks, for me. How if I found the right size (small enough to carry with me, big enough to be easy to browse back through when I'd filled it) and, for some reason, the right *color*, everything in them would turn out fine, ease of writing attaching to the tools I was using, and the pages would easily fill with ideas for short stories and novels, drafts of paragraphs and scraps of overheard conversations, stray lines of poems, words I'd discovered, quotes I liked, diary fragments, and dumb sketches…

70 SHEETS

10.5 x 8 in / 26.6 x 20.3 cm

1 SUBJECT NOTEBOOK

COLLEGE RULED

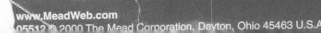

O O O o o o o o o o o o o

Jill Dawson
Seahorses

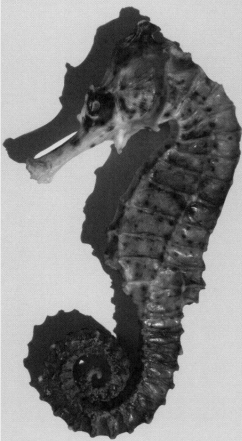

Photo by Meredith Bowles

It's 1997. I'm waiting for the school bus with my son and making small talk with another mother. I've already run out of "what grade is your son in?" openers. This is America, I'm a visiting Fellow, and I've no idea what grade my own son is in, anyway. "What do you do?" I ask her, glad to shift attention away from the kids. She says her name is Heather and she's researching the parenting styles of seahorses, here at Amherst College. Would I like to see them?

The next day she brings me a copy of *The Boston Globe*. She's not just any old seahorse researcher: she's Dr. Heather Masonjones, eminent marine biologist. She probably knows more than anyone in the world about the parenting style of seahorses. I cut the article out and file it. I haven't written *Fred & Edie* (my third novel) yet, nor even dreamed up *Wild Boy* (my fourth) but somehow I know that Heather—a morphed version of her—is going to end up in a novel. And that seahorses will be in there too.

The "first little throb," Nabokov called it, referring to *Lolita*. Something we know we can't use right now, but we recognize as a seed. Skip to 2003, and the new novel has a handful of images—a shark, a missing girl, the sound of a child bouncing a ball in a lane. I'm back in England. Googling "Heather" and "seahorses" uncovers a second amazing woman: Dr. Heather Koldeway, senior curator at London Zoo. Another Heather. Another world expert. I email her and she invites me to the zoo to meet the seahorses.

When I get there the aquarium needs a refit and bubbles like Frankenstein's lab. Heather's team are drinking coffee; in the middle of a briefing. They are all men, with bristling radios and green tracksuits. They are amused at me, a novelist, coming to interview Heather. "What's your novel about then?"

they want to know. "It's about girls. A girl goes missing in the '70s and her best friend tries to reconstruct what might have happened to her, thirty years later," I say.

"What have seahorses got to do with it?"

A good question. It's only a certainty I have that Tina, my protagonist, would feel passionate about them. I just want to look at them in fact, with no particular agenda. I pretend a whole list of questions to Heather but in fact I've hardly any.

"Why do you love them so much?" I ask. Heather says: "Well, they often live in places with treacherous currents. They have an amazing ability to camouflage by changing color. Their only defense mechanism is to blend into the background and hold on tight. That's poignant."

When I leave, Heather gives me two dried seahorses. They smell of seaweed and have fine snouts; their nose and cheek spines are still intact. They're crispy, like twigs. Now they're on my wall, stuck with Blu-Tack. The novel (*Watch Me Disappear*) was published in 2006, so that's nine whole years from the seahorses' first arrival in my life. They represent inspiration and chance, and connectedness. But mostly they remind me to be patient and to trust my instincts.

Chip Kidd

Quark

I am embarrassed to admit that since my first novel (which I began in 1995) I do ALL my writing—fiction or non—in Quark. When I tell this to a roomful of graphic designers at a lecture, they all burst into howls of derisive laughter. Quark, as you may or may not know, is a page layout and typesetting program. To use it as I do is the architectural equivalent of constructing the façade of a building first, and then the interior, then the plumbing and electrical work, and finally the foundation. It's completely backward.

How (I) Write + + + + + + + ONE HUNDRED AND FIFTY-EIGHT

Work
e Disk
Transfer
Font
4_CKidd
line CKidd
DS
My Auto Conve.

Desktop
ckidd
Applications
Documents
Chip
Fall 06
Spring 06
Summer 06
Vertical
Spring 07

X: 1.25"   W: 5.875"   0°   18 pt   12 pt

Quark is the last step in the publishing process; it's what you flow all of the text into once the final draft of something has been completely copyedited, so it can then be designed—set in type with proper margins, running heads, folios, etc.

So, whatever I write appears automatically finished—in the exact font, precisely placed. Which is of course why I love it. But it breeds a fiendishly false sense of security and bad writing habits. I have literally rewritten entire paragraphs just so the lines will break properly, something Nabokov would no doubt consider nothing less than a psychotic illness. When I delivered the first draft of *The Cheese Monkeys* to my editor at Scribner, her eyebrows went skyward and she remarked that it was the first manuscript she'd ever received in her life that appeared to have been already published. I should also add that regardless, she line-edited my prose with the zeal of a sugar cane farmer slashing and burning her way through a field of fiery stalks. And God bless her for it.

It's ridiculous, really, but at this point I'm so completely dependent on Quark I literally cannot write so much as an I.O.U. without my laptop. Which also means that a lot of the time I simply don't write, which is NOT a good thing. But the allure of instantly type-set prose is too enticing to resist. Once when I was at a publishing party I casually mentioned this to the writer Thomas Harris (*Silence of the Lambs*, *Hannibal*, etc.) and his face exploded in awed admiration. "I would LOVE to write like that," he roared, then thought a moment and added, "Then again, I'd probably never get anything done. I'd be too busy fiddling with the letterspacing."

Which goes a long way to explain why he's well into his fifth novel, and I'm still struggling with my second.

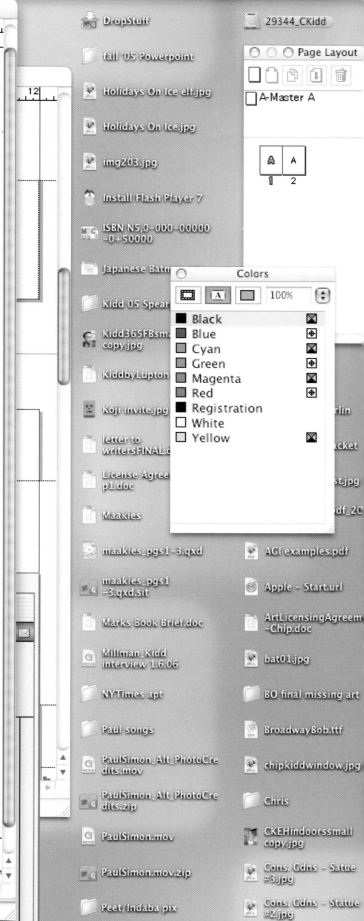

°Caren Beilin
"Office"

Here are some of the offices I've had,
like a list of lovers uttered dryly.

A crate.

A drum stand and a glass disk and a plastic chair the color of the sea if life listened to the proposals of the color wheel.

A low white coffee table and a red sofa, richer days.

One leaf of a dining room table one summer with no air-conditioner, near a shoebox stove that never quite turned off.

A "Writer's Desk" that came in a wide, flat box and the shortest screws I've ever seen. It had a slide-out keyboard tray, which was so archaic. Keyboards, in this particular first world on one of its rose-colored days, go in the donation bin swaddled by factory fresh yet slightly fucked-up diapers.

How a lover who lists might not have loved, I've never written in any of the places I've set up for writing. I cheated on them voraciously at the kitchen sink, on the train, during every math lecture I've ever been to, plotting language on the graph, in bed, that most traditional of cheating grounds. I've tried to stay where I was. I put *Leaves of Grass* on the desk, one of those writers who decides on a bible. I stockpiled Post-it notes; they would—I really hoped—stick my plots to the wall—I'd seen it on TV. I taped up a picture of Beckett after I realized my plots, in ways metaphorical, wouldn't stick. I faced a window. I swiveled. I faced a wall. I changed chairs. I couldn't swivel. I've seen ivy leaves shiver.

I saw the whole spectacular Chicago skyline from that red couch in richer days. Water towers were black as propaganda-style photos of extreme smokers lung. Looking up from that obsolete sandalwood tray, I watched my landlord's wife ascend and descend the porch stairs in new outfits, her pants flickering back and forth in the middle of the afternoon. But I never wrote much.

This is where I write—a small space behind the bathroom. I'm cheating on a jumble of furniture downstairs to write up here. I like to sit up against the water heater. I've been wondering about calling it Office. Take it seriously. I'm like one of those men who actually consider marrying their mistress, which, according to pop culture and the personal anecdotes of friends, due to weakness which festers, rarely ends up happening.

John Byrne
Typewriter

For writing my plays I currently use an Olympia "De Luxe" portable typewriter—bought in Sausalito for $11 about 5 years ago. It is my 27th or 28th such portable (different makes such as Hermes, Brother, Remington, etc.) but this one is the best. It is presently sitting on a slanted board on the counter of my writing "coffin"—an 8' x 4' room on the ground floor of our house (the limited space suits me admirably—the ideas can't fly out the small window but float around my head 'til I snatch them and stick them in the script). God bless the man who made it!

Nat Segnit
Barricade

Wherever I write I build a barricade of books around my computer. The psychology of this is as obvious as it is uncomfortable to admit. I like to think of my writing as an essentially calm and open hearted attempt to reveal something of myself on the page. The truth of it is I write like someone is standing there patting a baseball bat in their upturned palm muttering at me to write something now or give up.

As a largely unpublished writer I may be especially prone to this siege mentality. When your published oeuvre extends to two short stories in a now-defunct newspaper supplement it can be hard to banish the feeling that spending two hours trying to find a way not to repeat the word "listened" in an adjacent sentence without resorting to elegant variation might be an indulgence worthy of violent rebuke or remedial measure. Banishing this feeling, or at least holding the fort of my writerly self-esteem against it, is half the work of my book-barricade. Aside from the physical reassurance of being walled-in something like a corroborating principle of reverse influence obtains.

Here's how it works. The barricade is built of books that have had some influence on my writing. And if this influence proceeds from something in the writer's prose or world-view I admire, then in admiring my writing on the basis that it at least partially shares their world-view or taste for certain prose-rhythms, these writers must be influenced by me. It's entirely nuts of course, but if anything helps muster the presumptuousness you need to sit down, crack your fingers, and demand the attention of a putative readership, then that's okay by me.

For all its totemic function the barricade is first and foremost a reference tool. When my prose runs aground in complication it can help to pick up *Infinite Jest* or *American Pastoral* and see how a sentence stressed in all the right places can without sacrificing legibility go on for clause after clause, gathering in its reach across decades or states of mind such a weight of human information that the reader is moved in proportion to the distance the sentence has traveled. It's not that I could or would ever want to take anything directly from the writers I gather around me. There are books I love that owe their absence from the barricade to the ineradicability of their music from the mind. No use reading *Money* and trying to think in your own voice afterward. It's that there are certain books— like *CivilWarLand in Bad Decline*, and *The Quantity Theory of Insanity*, and *Humboldt's Gift*—that induce in me such a panicky sort of delight that the only thing I can do to calm myself down is write something of my own. It's a defense against having nothing to say, I guess, my book-barricade, but as it goes with defense, it works best when it goads me to get on with it.

Dan Rhodes
Rock Bottom

A couple of books in, it was clear that the plan hadn't worked. I should have been a celebrated *enfant terrible*, dominating bestseller lists the world over, married to Hope Sandoval (or Sabrina the Teenage Witch, I'd have been happy with either) and dividing my time between our West Village loft and our organic smallholding in the Wye Valley, but instead I was living, alone, in a studio flat at the top of Frant Road in Tunbridge Wells, working in the stockroom of a bookshop by day and writing a bleak novel about a man and his dog by night—a novel of which my publisher thought so little that they decided they weren't going to bother putting it out or paying me for it.

As battle commenced, a tax bill arrived. Cleaned out, I counted the contents of my penny jar. To the undisguised disgust of the man at the off licence, I paid for my eight-cans-for-a-fiver deals with handfuls of five-pence pieces. Hoping, in vain as it turned out, not to get fined for going over my overdraft limit, I put all my one-pence pieces into a sock, and all my two-pence pieces into another sock, and handed them to a sour-faced NatWest cashier. When I turned around, clutching my empty socks and hoping they weren't stretched so far out of shape that I wouldn't be able to wear them again, I was dazzled by the unexpected sight of Heavenli Abdi, one third of the chartbusting pop trio The Honeyz. She was doing an immaculate job of living up to her name as she stood in between the information desk and the ATM. My heart implored me to build my world around her, but how could I? I couldn't even afford to invite her to Goodman's Fish Bar on Camden Road for veggie chicken nuggets and chips (but not onions— Heavenli doesn't like onions). How could I possibly win her devotion? Our eyes met for a moment, and I could tell she knew exactly why I was holding a pair of socks. This wasn't how it was meant to be.

With the penny jar empty I was in the unenviable, but all too commonplace, position of being driven to drink while not being able to afford the drink to which I was being driven. I was flashing back into my pan without even having flashed out of it in the first place, but all the time there was a beacon of hope. In a clip frame on the wall by my desk hung a five-pound note that had been signed by David St. Hubbins from Spinal Tap. Not once did that fiver call to me, not once was I tempted to unclip the frame and spend it on eight cans of lager. Whenever I looked at it, and I looked at it every day, I knew I hadn't hit rock bottom, at least not yet. With a stroke of his pen, David Ivor St. Hubbins had given me the gift of perspective.

Things got better in the end. A lot better. I don't need the fiver so much these days, but it's still a part of my life, standing sentry between me and ruin. Last Thursday I took it from its frame, and out into the night. Derek Smalls was in town and his signature, given as graciously as you would expect, now sits proudly alongside David's. And I will do exactly as the man says.

I will rock on.

A.M. Homes
Hotel Rooms

Stage set. A tree; I cannot write without the view of a tree. And light, I cannot write without natural light. And Leonard Cohen, and Jimi Hendrix, and Glenn Gould, and Richard Yates to keep me honest, and John Cheever to keep me surreal, and Nabokov to make me work harder (and wish I were smarter). And honestly, the two places I work best—are not in my everyday life but outside of it.

Number one is Yaddo, the artist's colony in Saratoga Springs, New York—where I first went in 1989 just before my novel *Jack* came out. Yaddo is a place whose history itself is inspiring (think Pulitzer prize winners, think a little sex and a little scandal) and a community of artists—all working day and night, suspended from the demands and the dullness of everyday routine. My favorite room is not so highly prized, not the most perfect, but two rooms at the back of the house, above the staff entrance and over the kitchen. It's a big bedroom with a small writing studio attached. I wake up and go directly to work—and equally quickly do I leave, close the door behind me, and collapse onto a bed big enough to be filled with books—volumes to dream on. I like this part of the house because it wakes up early—the cooks arrive between 6 and 7 a.m. to make breakfast and lunches for the 30-odd guests. I hear them down below—a perfect distant murmur, enough to stimulate and inspire me—the sublime combination of alone but not really alone that hearkens back to my childhood: lying on my bed, looking out at the trees, daydreaming while my parents argue in the near distance, or sitting in the backseat of the car at night while my parents drive us home from the beach—a perfect, sun-baked, mindful, and mindless attending.

And as sublime as Yaddo is—and pure in that it is only an artist's colony—I find a similar creative inspirational vortex—like a time warp, a beautiful black hole—at the Chateau Marmont in Los Angeles. Eloise had the Plaza, Nabokov had the Montreux Palace Hotel, Hemingway had Harry's Bar, and I have the Chateau with its warped patina—half prestige, half psychosis. It is home away from home—better than home because there is room service and a housekeeper and a beautiful blue pool and the subversive smog of this strange city and a lobby filled with starlets. It is the perfect place to daydream. Here too there are spots for inspiration—my favorite room (all of the rooms are not just rooms, they are apartments with full kitchens, etc.) features grand piano and a terrace that allows one to eavesdrop on the guests dining below in the garden. The terrace allows one to see without being seen, it allows one to write, day or night it allows one to exist indoors and out and it is that rare place in a city of pretense and pretend where I can most be myself.

DBC Pierre
Tobacco

Dope is good for thinking about writing.
Pottering and playing, but not plotting.
Tobacco is the ultimate writing vice, a reminder
that nothing kills you as quickly as art. Cigarettes
let you know that if you could quit art, and
simply smoke to excess for fun, you would live
a rosy long life like a virgin athlete. But then,
what fucker wants to do that?

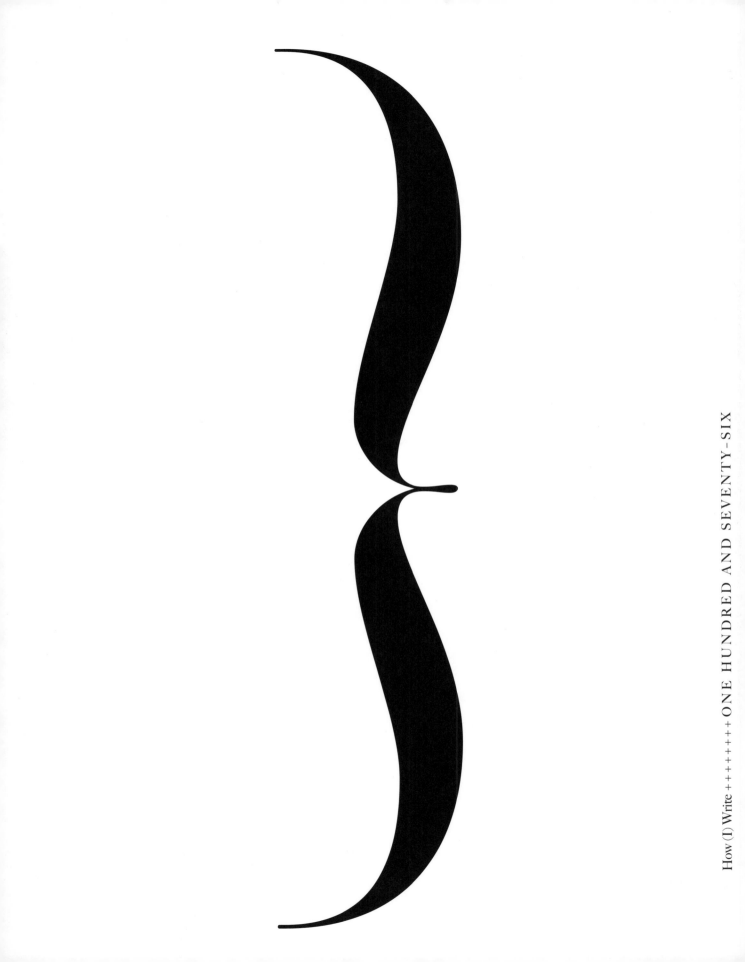

Biographies

ERIC CHASE ANDERSON was born in 1973. His illustration work has appeared in *Time*, the *New York Observer* and the movie *The Royal Tenenbaums*, which was directed by his brother Wes. In his early twenties, Eric drew a map in order to help him plot a novel and ended up becoming a professional mapmaker. In 2005 he went full circle and published his first novel, *Chuck Dugan is AWOL: A Novel with Maps*. JAKE ARNOTT was born in 1961. Having left school at 16 he drifted through various jobs, including a laborer, a mortuary technician, and an artist's model. He also became an actor with the Red Ladder Company in Leeds and appeared as a mummy in the Hollywood blockbuster *The Mummy*. His first novel, *The Long Firm* (1999), a story of 1960s gangland violence, has been filmed for BBC Television. His second novel, *He Kills Coppers* (2001), is about the brutal murder of three policemen, set in 1966, and his third novel is *Truecrime* (2003), a story of drugs, thugs, and revenge, set in the 1990s. Jake Arnott's most recent book is *Johnny Come Home* (2006). TASH AW was born in 1973. He grew up in Taiwan and Malaysia before moving to England in his teens. After graduating from Cambridge University, he worked at a law firm for five years, but then quit his job to pursue a writing career. While writing the book that would eventually win him the Whitbread First Novel Award—*The Harmony Silk Factory* (2005)—Tash worked as a gardener to pay a living. He lives in London but has a four square foot garden in which he still keeps all manner of exotic sub-tropical plants. DAVID BADDIEL was born in 1964. He studied English at Kings College, Cambridge, where he was also a vice president of the comedy club Footlights. On leaving, he performed stand-up on the London circuit while working on his Ph.D. First making himself a name with the *Mary Whitehouse Experience*—a radio series which moved to television—he went on to author three novels and now writes a regular column for the London *Times*. NICHOLSON BAKER was born in 1957. He attended the Eastman School of Music and Harvard University. Nicholson has established himself as one of the most brilliant observers of everyday experience. His first book, *The Mezzanine* (1989), changed the way people look at shoelaces and milk carton straws. Apart from writing novels, he has been a fervent critic of the destruction of paper-based media, specifically the elimination of material from libraries in the U.S. His book on this subject, *Double Fold*, won the National Book Critics Award in 2001. He has probably used more footnotes in his work than any other contemporary novelist. MELISSA BANK was born in 1960. During the 12 years it took her to write her first novel, she was moonlighting as a copywriter and refusing promotions in order to stay in a writing job. The result of her labors, *The Girls' Guide to Hunting and Fishing* (2000), won her international acclaim: her style has been described as a funnier John Cheever or a thinking woman's Bridget Jones. Melissa feels ambivalent about the "chick lit" bracket: "In the Victorian Age they categorized women writers as writing ladies' books. I feel like this is the same thing." Her latest novel is *The Wonder Spot* (2005). CAREN BEILIN was born in 1983. She is the only as-of-yet-unpublished author in this book. She says her life so far can be summed up by a short Lawrence Ferlenghetti poem: "See it was like this when we waltz into this place / a couple of papish cats is doing an Aztec two-step / and I says Dad let's cut/ but then this dame comes up behind me and says / You and me could really exist / wow I says / only the next day she's got bad breath and really hates poetry." She lives in Philadelphia and has been published in several literary journals. RONAN BENNETT was born in 1956. Aged 18 and still a schoolboy, he was arrested and charged with the killing of a Royal Ulster Constabulary officer during the course of an IRA bank robbery in 1974. His conviction was eventually overturned on appeal. Bennett moved to London to complete a Ph.D in history and ended up becoming a novelist. His most acclaimed works are *The Catastrophist* (1999), *Havoc In Its Third Year* (2004), and the screenplays for *Rebel Heart* and *Hamburg Cell*, a TV drama about the men who plotted and carried out the 9/11 attacks. ALAIN DE BOTTON was born in 1969. He was educated at Cambridge University, where he studied history. He is the author of several works of non-fiction, including the best selling *How Proust Can Change Your Life* (1997), an intriguing view of the French novelist's life, work, and influence that is at once an unlikely self-help guide and an introduction to one of the twentieth century's greatest writers. In February 2003, de Botton was made a Chevalier dans l'Ordre des Arts et des Lettres, one of France's highest artistic honors. ANTHONY BOURDAIN was born in 1956. He is the executive chef at Brasserie Les Halles in New York, and has spent more than two decades working in professional kitchens. His memoir/rant, *Kitchen Confidential* (2001), stemmed from an article he wrote for the *New Yorker* magazine about life behind the scenes in restaurant kitchens. The book described life in those kitchens in lurid detail and became a international surprise bestseller. He is also the author of two satirical thrillers, *Gone Bamboo* (1997) and *Bone In the Throat* (2000), as well as the urban historical *Typhoid Mary* (2001). ARTHUR BRADFORD was born in 1973. An original new voice in contemporary fiction, he writes dialogue that has an idiosyncratic, Jim Jarmusch-esque quality. His first book, a collection of stories called *Dogwalker* (2001), won over dog lovers and book critics alike. Bradford is most often praised for his characters—loopy oddballs that bring to mind Denis Johnson's more affable eccentrics. Arthur also directed *How's Your News?*, a celebrated road-documentary featuring Downs Syndrome and Cerebral Palsy sufferers driving across America interviewing strangers. ANTONIA SUSAN BYATT was born in 1936. "One is so much richer for being a great number of people," she once wrote. A.S. Byatt has been, among other things, an academic, a critic, a full-time novelist, a Booker Prize Winner (for *Possession*), the older sister of the novelist Margaret Drabble, a fierce critic of the Harry Potter books, a staunch defender of the fantasy writer Terry Pratchett, and the recipient of a DBE, in 1999. JOHN BYRNE was born in 1940. Aged 17, John started his first job as a "slab boy" in Glasgow, mixing dyes for a firm of carpet manufacturers in Paisley in what he describes as a "technicolor hell hole." He went to study art and soon became feted as one of the most promising Scottish artists of his generation. As a hoax, he once submitted a series of primitive paintings to a London gallery pretending that they were by his father Patrick. The gallery exhibited the work with great success. He is also an eminent playwright: his play *The Slab Boys* (1978) won him several awards and was put on in New York in 1993 with Sean Penn, Val Kilmer, and Kevin Bacon in starring roles. TIM CARVELL was born in 1973. He is a writer for *The Daily Show with Jon Stewart*, where he has won two Emmys. His writing has also appeared in *MAD*, *Esquire*, *Fortune*, the *New York Times*, and *McSweeney's*. He lives in New York. DOUGLAS COUPLAND was born in 1961. He once found himself introduced at a reading with the words "Mr. Coupland is German and once did an advertisement for Smirnoff vodka. He collects meteorites and lives in Scotland in a house with no furniture." Most of these facts are untrue. However, he has since started collecting meteorites. True facts about Douglas Coupland's life are that he has written nine novels, the first of which coined the phrase "Generation X," that he has also written several books of non-fiction about art and pop culture, that he has scripted the Canadian comedy *Everything's Gone Green*, and that he once chewed his own books and wove them into wasps nests. MARIE DARRIEUSSECQ was born in 1969. She wrote her first novel within six weeks while working on her Ph.D dissertation: *Pig Tales* (1996) is a Kafkaesque tale of shapeshifting in which a woman slowly transforms into a pig. The novel was accepted within 24 hours of being sent to a publisher and won her international acclaim. Marie lives in Paris with her husband, who is an astrophysicist. When we asked her to take a picture for this book, she apologized: "My husband's got the camera, and he's gone to the South Pole. It's true." JILL DAWSON was born in 1962. She first won major critical acclaim with *Fred and Edie* (2000), a novel based on the historic murder trial of Thompson and Bywaters. Her most recent book, *Watch Me Disappear* (2006), deals with another criminal case study. This time, the story is much closer to home: in August 2002, two girls went missing from Soham, a small town only a few miles from where Jill Dawson lives with two children and her husband, the RIBA-winning architect Meredith Bowles. JANINE DI GIOVANNI was born in the late sixties at the end of April. She is one of Europe's most respected reporters, with vast experience in covering war and conflict. She has been called the "the finest foreign correspondent of our generation." She has won four major awards, including the National Magazine Award—one of America's most prestigious prizes in journalism. She is a writer for the *Times* of London, *Vanity Fair*, the *New York Times Magazine*, the *Spectator,* and many others. On the matter of writing she has said: "When I wrote fiction at the Iowa Writers' Workshop I had nothing but my IBM Selectric typewriter for luck. But reporting war and conflict made me more superstitious." She lives in Paris. TONY D'SOUZA was born in 1974. From 2002 to 2003, he served as a rural AIDS educator with the U.S. peace corps in the Ivory Coast and Madagascar—experiences that inspired his first novel, *Whiteman* (2006): "My stories are an amalgam of non-sequential experiences coupled with events I wish had happened but didn't." His stories have appeared widely in magazines such as the *New Yorker, Stand, McSweeney's,* and *Playboy.* GEOFF DYER was born in 1958. Geoff's interests range widely—an article in the San Francisco *Chronicle* once compared him to "the brilliant, bored kid in class who can never bring himself to follow the assignment." With a trademark style that blends fiction, reportage, literary criticism, and travel writing, Dyer has written books about his hero John Berger (*Ways of Telling*, 1986), jazz (*But Beautiful*, 1991), D.H. Lawrence (*Out of Sheer Rage*, 1997), French bohemia (*Paris Trance*, 1998), globetrotting (*Yoga for People Who Can't Be Bothered to Do It*, 2003), and American photography (*The Ongoing Moment*, 2005). MICHEL FABER was born in 1960. In 1967 his family moved from Holland to Australia. Now he is staying put: since 1992 he has lived in a functioning Scottish train station. His short story "Fish" won the Macallan/Scotland on Sunday Short Story Competition in 1996 and is included in his first collection of short stories, *Some Rain Must Fall and Other Stories* (1998), winner of the Saltire Society Scottish First Book of the Year. His grand Victorian novel *The Crimson Petal and the White*, full of sex, moral collapse, and redemption, became a bestseller in 2002. He has recently said that he has only one more novel in him, which is a great pity. JAMES FLINT was born in 1968. He studied philosophy and psychology at Wadham College, Oxford, and has worked as an editor for *Wired UK* and *Mute* magazine. *Habitus*, his first novel, was judged to be among the top five foreign novels of 1992 in France's rentrée litteraire. *Time Out London* called it "probably the best British fiction début of the last five years." It is now published in Gallimard's classic *Folio Editions*, number 4092. *The Book of Ash* (2004) won an Arts Council Writers' Award. WILLIAM FIENNES was born in 1970. At the age of 25, he fell seriously ill. One of the things that helped him through a long and dark period of convalescence was a book he had first read as a child, *The Snow Goose* by Paul Gallico. "I was excited about something for the first time since I'd fallen ill, and I needed a project, a distraction, a means of escape." The distraction turned into a book: *The Snow Geese* (2002) charts Fiennes's journey with the birds from Texas to Baffin Island, Canada, beautifully blending biography, natural history, and philosophy. TIBOR FISCHER was born in 1959. His Hungarian parents were both professional basketball players who had left Hungary in 1956. His first novel, *Under the Frog* (1992), originally titled *Under the Frog's Ass*, won the Betty Trask Award. He lives in London. JONATHAN FRANZEN was born in 1959. In 2001 he was disinvited from the Oprah Winfrey book club show after expressing his disapproval of stickers bearing the program's logo appearing on his novel *The Corrections*. The evolving controversy has overshadowed his merit as a writer. His first two novels, *The Twenty-Seventh City* (1988) and *Strong Motion* (1992), still openly displayed a reverence to European writers such as Franz Kafka and Karl Kraus—but with *The Corrections* he arguably delivered the first great American novel of the 21st century. In his memoir *The Discomfort Zone* (2006) he writes passionately and sensitively about death, divorce, birdwatching, and the Peanuts cartoons. DAVID GUTERSON was born in 1956. He used to be a high-school teacher, but must have found something about it terrifying. When Guterson's own children started going to school, he and his wife started having anxiety attacks. He decided to teach his children at home and wrote an enlightened book about it, *Family Matters: Why Homeschooling Makes Sense* (1992). This was before he wrote *Snow Falling on Cedars*, his bestselling novel of love and war set in the Pacific Northwest, which went on to win him a PEN/Faulkner Award in 1994. PETER HOBBS was born in 1973. Growing up in Cornwall and Yorkshire, he studied International Relations at Oxford, and would have been a diplomat by now but for the intervention of a tropical illness or three. He is convinced that *The Short Day Dying* (2005), the story of a Methodist lay preacher set in 1870s Cornwall, must be the untrendiest debut novel ever published by a trendy young novelist. His first short story, "Malone Dies," was published in *Zembla* magazine in 2004—a collection of his short fiction with the title *I Could Ride All Day in My Cool Blue Train* followed in 2006. ALAN HOLLINGHURST was born in 1954. "How mad the hetero world is," ponders one of the characters in *The Swimming-Pool Library* (1988). At Oxford University Alan Hollinghurst visited the same college as Oscar Wilde, but unlike the 19th-century playwright he has never had to disguise the homoerotic subject matter in his fiction. *The Swimming-Pool Library*, *The Folding Star* (1993), *The Spell* (1998), and *The Line of Beauty* (2004) form a quartet of books about gay life in 1980s England. For the latter Hollinghurst received the Booker Prize in 2005. AMY MICHAEL HOMES was born in 1961. She is the author of six novels, the short story collections *The Safety of Objects* (1990) and *Things You Should Know* (2002), a travel book about Los Angeles and the artist book *Appendix A* (1996). "If Oprah went insane," said John Waters about *This Book Will Save Your Life* (2006), "this might be her favorite book." A.M. Homes lives in New York. SIRI HUSTVEDT was born in 1955. There are several fascinating things to be said about Siri apart form the fact that she is married to the novelist Paul Auster. Such as that *What I Loved* (2003) established her as one of the most talented voices in contemporary fiction. That she is also an art critic and has published two collections of essays, *Mysteries of the Triangle* (2005) and *A Plea for Eros* (2005). That the title of her Ph.D thesis on Dickens was already as poetic as her later prose: *Figures of Dust. A Reading of Our Mutual Friend*. Or that when she was very young, she announced her decision to become a writer to her local newspaper. ALISON LOUISE KENNEDY was born in 1965. She studied English and drama at Warwick University, where she began writing dramatic monologues and short stories. Her novel *So I Am Glad* (1995) won the Encore Award. She is a Fellow of the Royal Society of Literature. In 2003 she was nominated by Granta magazine as one of 20 "Best of Young British Novelists." To relax she practices T'ai Chi sabre form. CHIP KIDD was born in 1964. Since joining Knopf in 1986, he has become the most influential book cover designer of his generation. He has created over 1,500 book jackets for writers such as David Sedaris, Frank Miller, John Updike, and Bret Easton Ellis—several of which are more memorable than the words between the covers. His most famous design is perhaps the T-Rex skeleton that was eventually used on the cinema posters for *Jurassic Park*. Author Michael Crichton sent a fax with the following words upon receiving the original cover sketch: "Wow! Fucking Fantastic Jacket." Chip's first novel, *The Cheese Monkeys*, was published in 2001. NICOLE KRAUSS was born in 1974. There are several fascinating things to be said about Nicole Krauss apart from the fact that she is married to the novelist Jonathan Safran Foer. That she completed her thesis at Oxford on the artist/collector Joseph Cornell. That her first novel, *Man Walks into a Room* (2003), has an excellent title. That her second novel, *The History of Love* (2005), has been translated into more than 25 languages. Or that as a child, she used to play a game called "office," in which she pretended to be a travel agent. HANIF KUREISHI was born in 1954. He has collaborated with the director Stephen Frears on a number of films, including *My Beautiful Launderette* (1985), which was nominated for an Academy Award, and *Sammy and Rosie Get Laid* (1988). His first novel, *The Buddha of Suburbia*, was published in 1990. It won the Whitbread First Novel Award and was produced by the BBC in 1993 as a four-part television series with a soundtrack by David Bowie. Kureishi has recently published a memoir (*My Ear at His Heart*, 2004) and is a respected cultural and political commentator on issues ranging from religion to rock'n'roll. NEIL LABUTE was born in 1963. Chad and Howard, the protagonists in his feel-bad movie *In the Company of Men* (1997), are white-collar frat-boys with black souls: "Let's go out and hurt someone." A directing, script- and short-story-writing multitasker, LaBute has been continually drawn to the subject of human evil, in films such as *Your Friends and Neighbors* (1998), plays like *Bash* (1999) and *The Mercy Seat* (2002), or his short stories, a collection of which was published in 2004. His film adaptation of A.S. Byatt's novel *Possession* (2002), featuring Gwyneth Paltrow and Aaron Eckhart, revealed a lighter touch, but with his remake of the British horror classic *The Wicker Man* (2006) LaBute returned to his morbid best. NICK LAIRD was born in 1975. There are several interesting things to be said about Nick Laird apart from the fact that he is married to the novelist Zadie Smith. That he was born in Northern Ireland, that he completed a degree at Cambridge University, and that he worked for several years at a law company before becoming a full-time writer—much like the protagonist in his first novel *Utterly Monkey* (2005). That his first poem was the elegant rhyme "Bouncy bouncy on the bed / Happy Couple / Me and Ted." That his first collection of poetry, *To a Fault*, was published in 2005 and reveals a tougher voice: "The pistol jammed and they kicked him over. / They could break his legs, they offered, / but he waited, and another gun was brought." JT LEROY was born in 1980, or was he? Various rumors suggest that the real JT Leroy is the novelist Dennis Cooper or the film director Gus Van Sant, that the effeminate young man impersonating JT in public is only an actor/actress, and that the novels *Sarah* (2000), *The Heart is Deceitful Above All Things* (2001), *Harold's End* (2004), and *Labor* (2006) were all written by JT's minder, Laura Albert aka "Speedie." Whoever "JT Leroy" may be, we enjoyed the text he/she submitted to *How I Write* and deemed it good enough for publication.

JONATHAN LETHEM was born in 1964. He has lived in Brooklyn, NY, and the San Francisco Bay Area, and the subjects of his fiction span accordingly from the East to the West Coast: from Chandleresque detective fiction in *Gun, with Occasional Music* and Philip K. Dick-like dystopian sci-fi in *Amnesia Moon* to black music, graffiti, and lonely nights in big cities in *Motherless Brooklyn* and the semi-autobiographical *The Fortress of Solitude*. He once wrote a short story with the following immortal opening sentence: "I was running in the New York Marathon with Lawrence Olivier and Dustin Hoffman and John Coltrane and Drew Barrymore, only Lawrence Olivier was riding a banana-yellow moped." JAVIER MARÍAS was born in 1951. He wrote his first novel, *The Dominions of the Wolf*, at the age of 17. Young Marías went on to become a prolific translator of, among others, Thomas Hardy, Robert Louis Stevenson, Vladimir Nabokov, and John Updike. His translation of Sterne's *Tristram Shandy* won the Spanish national award for translation in 1979. Eventually returning to original composition, Marías authored several internationally acclaimed novels, including *My Heart So White* (1992) and the gossipy, semi-autobiographical account of a Spanish lecturer's life at the University of Oxford, *All Souls* (1989). He is also, somewhat confusingly, the king of Redonda, an approximately 1 square mile big island in the West Indies. A.S. Byatt is one of his duchesses. BENJAMIN MARKOVITS was born in 1973. He grew up in Texas, London, and Berlin. He has worked, variously, as a teacher, an editor, and a professional basketball player. His reviews and essays have been published in the *Observer*, the *New York Times*, and the *London Review of Books*. He has written three novels: *The Syme Papers* (2004), *Either Side of Winter* (2005), and *Imposture* (2007). CLAIRE MESSUD was born in 1966. Her parents are Canadian and French-Algerian, and she has described the painstaking effort of learning English as a second language as "a whimsical medley of lower case and capital letters." She has published a collection of two novellas, *The Hunters* (2001), and three novels, *When the World Was Steady* (1995), *The Last Life* (1999), and *The Emperor's Children* (2006). Messud's wrestles with the ghost of language have so far been rewarded with two nominations for the PEN/Faulkner award. JAY MCINERNEY was born in 1955. When once asked in an interview if there was one thing he wanted to change about himself, he answered: "My tendency to get mistaken for Bret Easton Ellis." It's no big surprise: both authors have documented the cocaine culture of '80s New York in their work, with Ellis's debut *Less Than Zero* (1986) having benefited heavily from the hype around McInerney's zeitgeisty *Bright Lights, Big City* (1984). McInerney even has a walk-on part in Ellis's *Lunar Park* (2005). His latest books are *Bacchus and Me: Adventures in the Wine Cellar* (2002) and his novel about September 11, *The Good Life* (2006). RICK MOODY was born in 1961. His first novel, *Garden State* (1992), won the Pushcart Editor's Choice Award. He is perhaps best known for *The Ice Storm*, a chronicle of the dissolution of two suburban Connecticut families over Thanksgiving weekend in 1973, which was also made into a film starring Sigourney Weaver. His memoir *The Black Veil* (2002) won the PEN/Martha Albrand Award for the Art of the Memoir. His writing has appeared in the *New Yorker*, *Esquire*, the *Paris Review*, *Harper's*, and the *New York Times*. NATASHA MOSTERT is South African and grew up in Pretoria. She is the author of *The Midnight Side* (2000), *The Other Side of Silence* (2001), and *Windwalker* (2005). Her next book, *Season of the Witch*, a modern gothic thriller about techgnosis and the Art of Memory, will have an international launch in April 2007. Her political opinion pieces have been published in the *New York Times*, *Newsweek*, the *Times* (UK), and the *Independent*. Future goals include executing the perfect spinning backkick and coming face to face with a ghost. She lives in London.

AUDREY NIFFENEGGER was born in 1963. She is a professor in the Interdisciplinary Book Arts MFA Program at the Columbia College Chicago Center for Book and Paper Arts. Her first book was the graphic novel *The Three Incestuous Sisters*. Using aquatint, a quaint method involving zinc plates and baths of nitric acid, she took 14 years to produce ten copies. She shot to fame as a novelist with her immensely successful first "proper" novel, *The Time Traveller's Wife* (2004), which has already been included in a list of "future classics" by the UK publisher Vintage. JOYCE CAROL OATES was born in 1938. "Gutted like a fish," ponders Ian McCollough in *American Appetites* (1989), "What had she meant by that?" From her first novel *With a Shuddering Fall* (1965)—a book that grew out of the social turmoil of urban America in the Sixties—"JCO" has become an expert at gutting and filleting the American dream. She continues to do so with such miraculous productivity that some people believe she is actually three people: Joyce, Carol, and Oates. She has written mystery novels under the pseudonyms Rosamund Smith and Lauren Kelly. Her latest novel—a trademark blend of the sensational and the intellectual—is *Black Girl White Girl* (2006). GINA OCHSNER was born in the late 20th century. *The Necessary Grace to Fall* (2002), her first collection of short stories, won the Flannery O'Connor for Short Fiction and was published by University of Georgia Press. Her second collection, *People I Wanted to Be* (2005), continues a morbid fascination with the non-living and 14th-century Romanian history. ZZ PACKER was born in 1973. ZZ are not her initials, she just found that people could pronounce it more easily than her real Swahili name. Although intent on becoming an electrical engineer, she forsook MIT for Yale and is forever grateful that she did. Her first book was the short story collection *Drinking Coffee Elsewhere* (2003), which became a PEN / Faulkner finalist and a *New York Times* Notable Book. She currently lives in the San Francisco Bay Area with her husband and son. DBC PIERRE was born in 1961. He grew up in Australia, Mexico, and the UK, and now lives in Ireland. Born Peter Warren Finlay, the "DBC" part of his nom de plume stands for "Dirty But Clean." "Pierre" was a nickname bestowed on him by childhood friends after a cartoon character of that name. He has worked previously as a designer and an internationally published cartoonist, but is now devoting himself to writing. His debut novel, *Vernon God Little* (2003)—a dark satire set in the aftermath of a Texas high school massacre—was the winner of the 2003 Man Booker Prize for Fiction. His second novel, *Ludmila's Broken English*, was published in 2006. IAN RANKIN was born in 1960. Aged 12, he invented a pop group in his head and started writing their lyrics. The lyrics eventually became poems, the poems short stories, and the short stories the raw material for his bestselling Inspector Rebus novels. In 1988 Ian was elected a Hawthornden Fellow and won the 1992 Chandler-Fulbright Award, one of the world's most prestigious detective fiction prizes (funded by the estate of Raymond Chandler). Ian now divides his time between Edinburgh, London, and France. DAN RHODES was born in 1972. He has worked on a fruit and vegetable farm, in the stockroom of a book shop, behind the bar of his parents' pub, as a teacher in Ho Chi Minh City, and, sporadically, as a full-time writer. He has published five books: *Don't Tell Me the Truth About Love*, *Anthropology*, *Timoleon Vieta Come Home*, *The Little White Car* (writing as Danuta de Rhodes), and *Gold*. He saw the Smiths at Brixton Academy on 12th December 1986. He lives in Scotland. TOM ROBBINS was born in 1936. In his early teens he ran away to join the circus. Then he ran away from the circus to join the literary world and has been one of its bigger attractions ever since. His first novel, *Another Roadside Attraction* (1971), was a commercial flop but slowly turned into a cult book—urban legend has it that Elvis was reading it on the toilet when he died. His second, *Even Cowgirls Get the Blues* (1976), got turned into a film by director Gus Van Sant. His latest book is *Wild Ducks Flying Backward* (2005), a collection of reviews and essays. "At the circus I had to clean the algae off the back of the alligator with a mop. I think that nicely symbolizes what I have been doing ever since. I wipe the crud off this great beast we call America." BRUCE ROBINSON was born in 1946. He featured as a young boy in tights in Franco Zeffirelli's *Romeo and Juliet* (1968), wrote and directed the British cult film *Withnail and I* (1987), and garnered an Oscar nomination for his screenplay of *The Killing Fields* (1984). In 1998 he published his first novel, *The Peculiar Memories of Thomas Penman*. LUIS J. RODRIGUEZ was born in 1954. By age twelve, he was a veteran of East L.A. gang warfare. He witnessed countless shootings, beatings, and arrests and saw drugs, murder, and suicide claim friends and family members. After he managed to break free from the gang culture of the streets, he wrote his memoir *Always Running* as a warning for his young son. The book was first published in the aftermath of the Rodney King uprising in L.A., in 1993. Over the last 25 years, Luis has published several volumes of poetry and has conducted workshops and talks in prisons, juvenile facilities, homeless shelters, migrant camps, schools, and universities. NAT SEGNIT was born in 1971. His reviews, features, and short fiction have appeared in several journals and newspapers including *The Times* and *The Independent* on Sunday. He is the author of a play for Radio 4, *Dolphin Therapy*, and is currently working on his first novel. WILL SELF was born in 1961. He is known for his satirical, grotesque, and fantastic novels and short stories set in seemingly parallel universes. He has written for a variety of publications and is a regular broadcaster on television and radio. In 1997 he was sent to cover the electoral campaign of John Major by *The Observer*, but was subsequently fired from the newspaper after taking heroin on the Prime Minister's jet. *Cock and Bull* (1992), his first novel, is the story of a man and a woman who develop sexual organs of the opposite sex. ELIF SHAFAK was born in 1971. She has lived in Spain and Turkey and is currently an assistant professor at the University of Arizona. She has published five novels, most recently *The Saint of Incipient Insanities* (2004)—an English-language novel with a protagonist who is a Turkish expatriate in Boston – which has been translated back into her native Turkish. At a booksigning she was once approached by an undergraduate girl wearing a headscarf and her very unreligious, urban chic boyfriend. "We met in the pages of your book," they told her. LIONEL SHRIVER was born in 1957. She has never wanted to have children, and anxiety about motherhood pervades *We Need to Talk About Kevin* (2003), her Orange Prize–winning novel in which protagonist Eva Khatchadourian struggles to come to terms with her impenetrable and malevolent offspring. Shriver attended Columbia University and lived for many years in Belfast, Northern Ireland. She currently divides her time between London and New York. Apart from *Kevin*, she has published several novels, including *The Female of the Species* (1987), *A Perfectly Good Family* (1996), and *Double Fault* (1997). IAIN SINCLAIR was born in 1943. "The public autograph is an announcement of nothingness, abdication, the swift erasure of the envelope of identity," he writes in *Lights Out for the Territory*. A poet, filmmaker, novelist, and former cemetery gardener, Sinclair has always been fascinated by locations in which fictional places and actual geography overlap. In *London Orbital* (2002), Sinclair followed the M25, London's outer ring motorway, and recorded his experience. His most recent book, *Edge of the Orison* (2005), traces the steps of 19th-century poet John Clare into Essex. JANE SMILEY was born in 1949. She has written a number of very different books to critical acclaim. *A Thousand Acres*, a modern-day *King Lear* set on a Midwest farm, became a bestseller and won the Pulitzer Prize in 1992. *The Greenlanders* (1988) is a medieval saga, *Moo* (1995) a campus novel, and *Thirteen Ways of Looking at the Novel* (2006) a dazzling work of non-fiction which ends with a list of the 100 novels she read to prepare for the book. Jane owns several horses and believes that riding and writing have much in common: "With a horse, even if you have a bad ride, you want to get back on because it is so interesting. Same with novels." AHDAF SOUEIF was born in 1950. Educated in Egypt and England, she often writes her novels in both English and Arabic, depending on what language the dialogue calls for. *The Map of Love*, the story of an affair between an Englishwoman and an Egyptian nationalist set in Cairo in 1900, was nominated for the Booker Prize in 1999. She continues to write non-fiction: *Mezzaterra*, a collection of her essays on Egypt, Palestine, and global politics, was published in 2004. ADAM THIRLWELL was born in 1978. In 2003 he was included in Granta's list of Best Young Novelists before he had published his first novel. All the judges had to go by was an extract entitled "The Art of Fellatio." A fellow at All Soul's College, Oxford, Adam eventually delivered his debut novel *Politics* in late 2003, a self-consciously clever piece of writing devoted to the niceties of sexual embarrassment. He is also the deputy editor of the literary journal *Areté*. MATT THORNE was born in 1974. He was educated at Sidney Sussex College, Cambridge, and the University of St. Andrews. He is the author of six novels including *Eight Minutes Idle* (1999, Winner of an Encore Award) and *Cherry*, which was longlisted for the Man Booker Prize in 2004. He has also written three books for children and edited two anthologies, *All Hail the New Puritans* (2000) and *Croatian Nights* (2005). VENDELA VIDA was born in 1972. There are several fascinating things to be said about Vendela Vida apart from the fact that she is married to the author Dave Eggers. That after being an intern at the *Paris Review*, she published a non-fiction book on the initiation rites of American teenage girls—*Girls on the Verge*—that developed out of her master's thesis. That her second book, the novel *And Now You Can Go* was published in 2003 and is the first part of a trilogy. That she is the founding editor of *The Believer*. That she doesn't eat chocolates but likes salts and that her name translates as "sell the life" in Spanish. WILLY VLAUTIN was born in 1967. He is the singer/songwriter in the Americana band Richmond Fontaine. Vlautin's lyrical style—manifested most recently on *The Fitzgerald* (2005)—is precise, melancholy, and in keeping with the romantic idea in the American folklore tradition. Comparisons to Tom Waits, Raymond Carver, and Denis Johnson helped Vlautin gain publishing deals for his first novel in the U.S., the UK, and Australia. *The Motel Life* (2006) features the two brothers Frank and Jerry, Bluebeard the pirate, a dead duck, and no guitar players. LOUISA & ISABEL ADOMAKOH YOUNG were born in 1960 and 1993, respectively. They are mother and daughter. Together, they write under the pseudonym "Zizou Corder" (because both their names wouldn't have fit on the cover of a book). Zizu is the name of Isabel's pet lizard. They are the authors of the popular Lionboy-trilogy, in which young boy Charlie Ashanti discovers that he can talk to cats—a skill that becomes particularly useful when he meets a pride of six lions on a traveling circus boat and makes friends with them. Louisa and Isabel say they enjoy working together, even though Isabel fears that her mother might soon want to write a "grown-up novel" and that she herself might become a teenager and start sulking.

Acknowledgments
This book was edited in London, designed in Sydney, and published in New York. Special thanks to: Simon Finch, whose contribution was vital to the creation of the book, Joanna Biggs, Lauren Goldstein Crowe, Suzanne Dow, Philip Grey, Alex Griessmann, Vince Frost, Leo Hollis, Jonathan Heawood, Michel Krafft, Garrett Linn, Eamonn McCabe, Ivan Mulcahy, Tom Phillips, Simon Prosser, Jemma Read, Deborah Rogers, Rowan Routh, Studio8, Andrew Staffell, Minnie Weisz, Louise West, Hannah Westland, and to all the contributing writers who were willing to share their secrets.